MONROE COUNTY DEER HUNTS

Why the Good Old Methods Are Best

Keith Francis Organ

Published by Wheatmark®
2030 East Speedway Boulevard, Suite 106
Tucson, Arizona 85719 USA
www.wheatmark.com

ISBN: 979-8-88747-045-0
LCCN: 2023901436

Bulk ordering discounts are available through Wheatmark, Inc. For more information, email orders@wheatmark.com or call 1-888-934-0888.

*Sixty years of whitetail deer hunting
in Monroe County, Wisconsin.*

CONTENTS

FOREWORD

In my youth, you did not hear the traffic sounds from the concrete ribbons that now cut across our county. There were no all-terrain vehicles destroying the environment with each pass they made through the woods. People walked to places in the wild and felt connected to their surroundings. The woods were quiet, a classroom filled with many teachers waiting to show visitors the secrets of the wild.

Four-wheel drive vehicles were a luxury that most folks couldn't afford. Most vehicles stuck to the roads—leaving many areas of the county wild. There were unbroken corridors of wooded land, facilitating the migration of wild animals. Hunters willing to learn the ways of the wild country were rewarded with trophy bucks.

Boys were transformed into men by taking their first buck, a rite of passage into manhood. But, unfortunately, the sport has been ruined by the changing landscape. The development of sand mines, cranberry operations, plantation farms, and houses in the forest has forever spoiled much of the land for hunting.

New-age high-tech hunters entered the sport, building tree stands in the woods and creating deer feeding stations. Then they set up cameras to monitor each deer that comes to feed. I'm now afraid to take a pee in the woods. The event might end up on Facebook, and I'd be arrested for indecent exposure.

Fathers have now introduced their children to what I call a sit-about. He knows when the buck will show up, how many points he has, and where he'll come from. The children take turns sitting in their houses with cell phones, lunches, and hot cocoa, watching for a buck their father has been feeding for three months.

The kids know nothing about deer hunting and hate the taste of venison. Their biggest goal is to get a picture of their trophy on their cell phone for bragging rights. If they take a buck, the father will field dress it out for them. He then drives the pickup truck to the stand to load the buck. They'll hurry to the butcher to process the buck into sausage. The butcher will produce meat filled with chemicals and salt.

What would be wrong with learning to remove the hide, cut up, can, or cook venison correctly? Dad, if you don't like venison, why not use that time with your children to explore the woods? Maybe you'll find a hollow tree with honeybees in it or find a nest of flying squirrels. Have you ever thought of hunting with a camera? How about teaching your children the ways of the wild country? It would be a gift to them and indeed to the planet.

Sand mines and cranberry operators have driven the price of land up, making it too costly for poor folks to own. These operations are destroying our freshwater aquifers, turning them into chemical dumps and stripping the very sand needed to filter the water, and creating monocultures where beautiful, biodiverse watershed once laid.

The small parcels of land not controlled by these rich *Truth Deniers* are owned by self-appointed kings. They imagine that they are biologists correctly managing the deer herd. The deer belong to them as a herd of cows would belong to a farmer.

Deer hunting is no longer a sport for poor folks. Today, hunting more closely resembles a feedlot operation. Fatten the bucks up for the king's daughter to slaughter. This ridiculous way of baiting deer results in poor management of the herd. Shouldn't the taking of wild animals be about what's best for the resource?

In my time, you had to know how to read the signs of deer. What kind of cover did they prefer in different weather patterns? Which direction was the wind blowing, so you could plan your hunt from a downwind advantage? When to hunt the hill country or swampland. You had to study feed trails, buck rubs, and scrapes and know the patterns of deer.

We'd called it jump hunting when two hunters would try to flush a buck out to each other. Approaching the hunting area from different directions would give you or your hunting partner a shot at a buck. In my opinion hunting this way is the best way to take deer in a sporting fashion. No, cameras, corn piles, or unethical hunting practices. Who shoots the bucks doesn't matter; all share in the blessing.

I remember the days I'd walk fifteen miles through the woods to hunt deer. They call it a walkabout in Australia, a day when you just explore the wild. What was over the next ridge? Was it a sighting of a gray fox, or maybe you'd been surprised by a red-tailed hawk? Every valley had something new to show me as I traversed the forest.

If I could find soft pine needles, could I sneak up on a buck in his nest? There were fewer leaves on the steep grades of hog's backs just below the ridgeline; might I take advantage of that? It didn't matter if I saw deer; it was the wild drawing me into the next adventure. These walks left my body in incredible shape; the woods were also medicine for my soul.

I realized this after losing my ability to walk in the woods. In 1969, my left leg was amputated from injuries I suffered in combat. I was drafted, like most underclass boys not smart enough to avoid the Vietnam War. Since then, I've shot some nice bucks from natural ground blinds, but I still miss the walkabouts of my youth.

I hope you enjoy my stories of the walkabouts of my family's hunts in the once-beautiful Monroe County. Unlike the kings nowadays who believe they own the deer, my family earned our bucks by hunting like lions.

1

BULLWINKLE

It was 1963, and my brother-in-law Jim Martin had just picked me up from school to travel north for the deer hunt. I remember him telling me President John F. Kennedy had been shot in Dallas, Texas. I was in school at Washington Junior High School in Racine, Wisconsin.

When I got home to pick up my hunting gear, Mom had tears in her eyes from the news of the president's death. She loved the Kennedy family; they were Catholic, liberals, and best of all, Irish.

I grabbed a quick sandwich, my .30-.30 Winchester lever-action rifle, and the rest of my clothing. Within fifteen minutes, Jim's Delta Oldsmobile was closing the distance from Racine to Warrens, Wisconsin.

We were the first to arrive at deer camp, a trailer on a wooded lot close to our hunting grounds. We fired up the stove, unpacked our gear, and loaded our hunting clothes on the best bunks for our stay.

It wasn't too long before the rest of the gang pulled in. Everyone was upbeat, telling stories of seasons gone by, of the big bucks they had missed over the years.

Altogether there were eleven hunters, mostly family. A few friends also permanently joined us for the hunt.

The hunt would start early the following day. We turned in after a cup of coffee accompanied by a few slices of Danish kringle. It sounded like a band concert with all the farting in the small trailer. Someone would fart, then lay it on someone else. Laughter would follow. Gradually, the farting stopped, replaced by snoring. I was the last to fall asleep. The excitement for the coming hunt had me pumped up.

Thank God I awoke to the smell of bacon frying. The farts had dissipated. We didn't have a huge breakfast but always tried to eat a little more than cold cereal. I opened the trailer door, sticking my head out to see if we'd gotten any snow overnight. We'd picked up a couple of inches, which would help with tracking.

We always formed some game plan for the day. You know, the who, where, and what's of the hunt. We dressed in sheepskin vests, wool red and black plaid coats, long underwear, Levi's, and felt high-top boots.

My uncle lived on this farm. Early in the season, he had done some scouting for us. We'd decided to hunt the highland swamps west of his place. They were mainly hardwood with jack pine islands that grew after logging.

We knew the area well and took stands with enough open timber to shoot. Around 7:30, I heard shots east of my deer stand. Two four-point bucks almost ran over me. I got so excited I shot over them. The .30-.30 Winchester had a Buckhorn sight on it. You'd shoot over your target if you didn't get down in the groove. Oh, shit—I'd done it again.

The morning went by quickly. I shot at four more bucks, not touching one of them. It was around one o'clock in the afternoon, and I was out of shells. I decided to go back to the trailer to restock my shell belt. We had installed a meat pole between two large oak trees in front of the trailer.

When I turned the corner, nine bucks were hanging on the pole. Most were small bucks, but there were a few nice eight-pointers and one nine. We'd always done well the first day, but this was outstanding. I licked my wounds, retreating into the trailer.

Dad saw me trying to blend into the woodwork. "Did you see any?"

"Yes, I shot at five bucks, and I'm out of shells."

He laughed. "You want to use my gun?"

"No, it's my fault, not the gun's."

"Well, I can shoot one for you if you want."

"No, I've got the whole season to shoot one. I'll get one."

Dad was hunting with a .35 Remington Woodsmaster, which I hated. It had a barrel inside of the barrel. It was a heavy gun that was hard to load in cold weather. I never understood what he saw in the weapon. But if you heard him shoot, he'd have a buck down.

It was a buck-only season in those days. Bucks were usually smaller but better eating than the ones taken nowadays. Dad and my uncle Hipe could shoot deer on the run better than any man alive. They weren't that good at target shooting, but run a buck by them and they seldom missed.

The following day a friend named Bill Jacobs and I decided to do a little jump hunting. Bill had seen a few bucks on the opener but didn't connect. Uncle Hipe cut winter wood and piled brush in the swamp. He suggested we try that area because they'd hole up in the heavy cover after the open-day pressure.

A nice trout stream ran down the middle of the swamp. I circled to the west and cross the stream with a running jump. Saw a nice brook trout when I did. Bill stayed east of the stream. We had prearranged to meet a mile downstream.

I hunted slowly around the brush piles, often stopping to mimic the sounds of squirrels feeding. When I stopped, I always had my gun ready. Bucks will think you've spotted them if you stop for a few minutes. So I walked maybe a quarter mile, stopping to do my squirrel imitation.

A rack buck exploded from a brush pile about seventy-five yards in front of me. I raised my gun but could not get a clear shot. The buck bounded across the stream. In a few minutes, I heard Bill shoot. Another running jump, and I was back over the creek.

I walked in the direction of the shooting for around five hundred yards. Then, finally, the timber opened up with small brush piles spread out before me. Behind one of them, Bill sat with the biggest smile. He'd taken a nice seven-point buck.

This very woods where this hunt took place is now

the site of a cranberry marsh. They've dammed up the beautiful trout stream, cut down all the forest, and planted berries, which they dump chemicals on, contaminating the once pristine trout stream and forest.

Sad to say, this would be Bill's first and last buck he'd take. A few years later, he and his brother-in-law took two little girls to Sunday school. Bill was riding shotgun. They stopped for a train and let it pass, only to pull in front of another train coming from the opposite direction. All four of the passengers in the car had died.

We field dressed the buck and pulled him to a fire lane for pickup. I was the only one in the party who didn't have a buck hanging. I felt like I couldn't have hit a cow in a tunnel with a light in her ass. Bill reassured me that I would get one sooner or later.

Over the years, when I'd shoot a buck, I'd spend a few minutes reflecting on the day. Always quietly mouthing these words: "Bill, you were right, buddy." Little did he know, I'd see the biggest buck of my life this season.

My dad and the rest of the hunting party had to return to Racine to work their jobs the following morning, so I went to stay with Uncle Hipe and Aunt Margret. My brothers would return on Thanksgiving to hunt the rest of the week.

Hipe was a large man built for the woods, with a couple of strands of hair left on his head. He always wore bib overalls, long underwear, and high-top boots. The years of logging had seasoned his powerful body.

One draft horse can pull eight thousand pounds, and two draft horses can tow twenty-four thousand pounds. I believe Hipe could have pulled more than both draft horses. His favorite pastime was telling stories of the days he spent logging in the wilds of Wisconsin.

Aunt Margret was dad's younger sister. She had a dark complexion and black hair. Small features reminded me of the French women I met on my trips to Canada. She was a good-natured woman. She wore only dresses, usually with an apron over them. Staying with them was better than being home with my mother.

They always treated me like I was their son. Aunt Margret was a great cook. She baked on a wood stove. Of course, I'm talking about everything from scratch. If I close my eyes, I can still smell the fresh bread baking in that old wood stove. They were poor but very rich in their hearts, willing to share whatever they had with me.

That night it started to snow, and we had a few new inches by the following day. After a lumberjack breakfast, we hunted the swamps where Bill had shot his buck. It was around noon when we gave up, returning to the house.

The snow had continued that morning. Our clothing was wet, and the wool coats weren't the best for those conditions. We decided to take a break in the afternoon. Uncle Hipe hung our coats on a wooden rack by the woodstove to dry. We loaded up the wood box and did some chores for Aunt Margret.

He then started telling stories of his days working in the wilds of Wisconsin in the logging industry. He told stories of killing a black bear with an ax, of seeing wolves riding into his worksite. At times fights would break out in the only bar in the area, and he told of ladies of the night that worked the bar on Saturday nights after payday. Aunt Margret would give a disapproving glance in his direction, and he changed course.

I remember a song he used to sing to her. "The old red rooster said to the old red hen, 'I haven't had any since God knows when.' So, he ruffled up his feathers and shook his tail. 'I'm going to get a little if I have to go to jail.'"

Aunt Margret listened until he had finished, then remarked, "If you don't shave your face, it's the jail for you." Hipe's love for Margret was pure love infused with humor.

They shared their feelings freely. There weren't all the modern distractions that separate us today. Relationships took on a more critical role in life. People needed to share their lives with their mates.

The following day had turned cold, so we decided to stay in until after lunch. After eating lunch, Hipe devised a game plan for the afternoon. To the east of their property, it was hilly. About a mile from the house, there was a large, open abandoned farm field. The forest was mostly oak trees. In the late afternoon, deer would feed on the grasses in the field.

Old Joe was a retired farmer that lived with them. He was in his early eighties at the time, a slender, handsome man with a full head of white hair. Joe wore an oversized brim hat and chewed plug tobacco. He never married and lived with his mother until she passed.

Their farm was next to our place when I was a kid. He raised bees and sold honey. Other than day jobs, I don't think he ever worked for anyone else. He could make enough money to get by with a small farming operation. He drove a Model T Ford—now, boy, this was in the 1960s. That car lasted him his entire life. He hunted with a Winchester lever-action .25-.20 with a hexagon barrel.

He liked to fish trout, and he'd visit a couple of old maids after catching a mess. Rumor had it he provided the fish, and they'd give the company. I was told Joe was hung like a pony. I don't know where that started, but the guys always joked about it. Although, come to think about it, he never denied it.

Anyway, he wanted to come along for the afternoon hunt. He knew the woods. He did a lot of walkabouts picking blueberries and blackberries in the summer.

Not only did he know where the berries grew, he'd tell me why they grew on a particular hillside or what weather patterns they favored. His connection to the Monroe County woods was remarkable, and he knew most woods like one would know the back of his hand.

Hipe instructed him, "Wait fifteen minutes and then circle to the north. Bring the other side of the hogs back down to us." We beelined it to a hill overlooking the farm field. The field was flat with white grass and oak trees surrounding it.

Hipe said, "Set down a while before you walk to the other side of the field." So I did, and ten minutes passed. I was just about to get up when I saw a deer at the bottom of the hill.

It was Bullwinkle himself, the largest buck I've ever seen in over sixty years of hunting. The buck must have gone every bit of 275 pounds, with a magnificent rack. I'm talking way outside the ears with tines a foot long. I didn't count the tines, but I'm sure there were at least fourteen. The rack was very high with no drop tines.

He must have heard us talking. He turned, running straight away from us. Both of us raised our guns to shoot. I aimed my rifle at the big boy, and the bead on my .30-.30 Winchester covered his body. The target was smaller than my gun's bead, but I took a shot anyway.

Hipe's gun cracked right after, and the buck kept running, covering large distances with each bound. We stopped shooting. There was little chance that we'd connect at that distance.

The buck ran until he reached the other side of the field. He stopped just after entering the woods. There he stood for a few minutes before disappearing into the forest. I look at Hipe, remarking, "You know I was going to sit where he entered the woods."

Hipe asked me, "Would you have walked across that field?"

"Yes," I replied.

"He would have to pick up where you walked and never come to you. So you needed to circle downwind on top of this hill. See that thick finger of pine about halfway across the field?"

"Yes, I do."

"Well, that's your stand for this hunt. A lion would want to cut the chase in half. He also knows deer favor heavy cover this early in the day. Of course, he'd check the wind direction before committing to an ambush," Hipe said, punching me in the arm.

I said, "Old Joe did his job flushing the buck out to us. But, unfortunately, we were the ones dillying around instead of keeping our noses to the ground to finish the hunt. Dang it, we should be horsewhipped."

Hipe said, "Old Joe is a blueberry picker; he is not a lion. But maybe you'll take this buck's son or grandson on your hunts in the coming years."

I struggled to understand Hipe's attitude about the buck. It didn't matter to him that we'd missed our chance at Bullwinkle. "What if someone else shoots him?" I said.

Hipe said, "The buck belongs to the forest, as we do. So many blueberry pickers have seen him. It will take a lion to have him for supper."

My teacher had given me the fountain to think about hunting on a different level. I learned that if I were going to take a good buck, I'd have to understand the ways of the deer.

Hipe understood the connection to nature. He'd spent his life in the woods and was willing to share his knowledge with a young boy, so I listened carefully to him after that day, hoping I could learn the ways of the forest before the knowledge was lost.

Hipe, of course, has gone on to be with Jesus. Nowadays, Hipe's understanding of nature is taught by professors. Students searching for knowledge read books of the wild. Most of them couldn't find their peckers in a pickle jar.

If you want to be a lion, you have to go into the forest. Therefore, grad school requires time in nature. If you don't believe me, ask Jane Goodall if I'm right. Then, of course, like my uncle Hipe, you must teach the rest of the youth what you've learned.

2

PRETTY BOY

The following year, the gang had shrunk to nine hunt-ers. Bill, my best friend, had been grounded by his mother for pulling some stunt. His parents had gotten a divorce, and his mother, Marie, was doing her best to keep him in line.

I remember his father was one of the meanest SOBs I'd ever met. He had a German shorthaired pointer for hunting pheasants. After he got drunk, this was every day of the week, he'd make the dog stand at attention in front of him for over an hour. I felt so bad for the dog. I always wished the dog would take a piece out of the drunken bastard.

My father's friend Deep was also missing. He had to work overtime and couldn't get away from his job. Deep was an interesting guy. He was a tramp during the Depression. He told stories of traveling our country by hitching rides in boxcars. His stories of working hours for a sandwich and a cup of coffee were interesting.

One story I remember him telling me, it was during the Depression, and he'd gone west to Oregon to pick crops in the fields. He lived in a house built from cardboard boxes next to a ditch. He had no running water, electricity, or sanitation of any kind.

Many families with small children did the same thing. The children were wormy, full of head lice, and suffered from malnutrition. A few children died, and it got out to the press.

The wealthy crop growers took no responsibility for the children. The plantations formed when our country was founded reappeared during the Depression. It was the best of times for the rich and the worst for the poor. Of course, it looked terrible when the children started dying. Also, I'm sure the county didn't want pickers on their welfare rolls.

They must have asked the federal government or the state of Oregon to devise a plan to ship them back to the Midwest. They loaded the families in boxcars and sent them back to where they came from like a herd of cattle.

Growing up, we were poorer than church mice, but his stories of hard times would always shock me. I never realized just how bad things were during the Great Depression. So, the good old days weren't always that good.

He lived a nomadic lifestyle until he met his wife, Anne, an excellent Christian lady who settled him down. She insisted he go to church on Sundays. No swearing or drinking, and of course, he had to keep a steady job. They married, had two children, and spent the rest of their days together.

This year we'd not hunt on the farm for the first day. Instead, we traveled northeast of Warrens. Dad knew an area that was close to a cranberry marsh. He had raked berries for the owner in his younger days. I'm not sure, but maybe the party permit was for that area.

The marsh was full of small pines, and it was almost impossible to get a shot at a buck. The deer were there all right, but extremely difficult to shoot. My brothers and I saw bucks, but no one had any nut sacks on their belts. Floyd shot a doe to fill the party permit. I guess that answers the question as to why we hunted that swamp.

Dad was not in the best shape, so he sat along a tiny field close to the car. On our way back to the car, we kicked out a buck. Unfortunately, he made the mistake of crossing the area where Dad was sitting. Three shots rang out, and a nice ten-pointer lay dead when we got to the field.

Dad was always good at picking a suitable stand for the opener. Of course, it didn't hurt to have five sons to jump the bucks out of the heavy cover. Uncle Hipe did not go with us. He stayed home and hunted the hills to the east of his place. He also had no blood on the ground.

A lousy day for hunting. We had one buck and a party doe for nine hunters. We took the deer to town for registration. I liked looking at all the bucks the guys were bringing in for registration. An elderly lady was there with her son. I talked to her, and she told me they had a nice buck that fed in her garden. "Would you care if we hunted for him?" I asked.

"No, I'd like to get rid of the critter. Just don't shoot one of my sheep."

"No, I probably couldn't hit one anyway." I laughed. "Where are you folks located?"

"We're on County Road O, just after you get to the turnoff for Mosley's orchard."

Dad said, "I know that farm. I lived in the Warrens area growing up."

Well, that was all it took. *Do you know so and so? Yes, we're related to them. I used to go to school with them. Did you know my folks? I'll bet you went to the town hall dances*—this went on for fifteen to twenty minutes. Then, finally, the conversation died down between them.

"Dad, are you ready to go?"

"Yep, I've been waiting for you to stop dilly-dallying like some schoolgirl for fifteen minutes."

I rolled my eyes and gave him the "Oh really?" look. Then, I thanked the newfound friend my dad had made as I turned to go. "We'll give him a hunt tomorrow morning. I promise I won't shoot one of your lambs."

Dad said, "A couple of guys would be able to kick the woods in less than a half hour." So, my brother Joe decided to take me on the hunt. We headed out just after light and arrived early. We sat in the car for a few minutes to plan the hunt.

They had a long driveway with cropland and pasture to the south. The woods ran down the north side of the driveway around the back of the house. I could see two outbuildings and a barn.

Joe was to circle through the pasture to stay far enough from the woods not to spook him. So I followed the wood line down. Then, finally, I took a stand that cleared the house and barn for a shooting lane.

The ambush of the buck was ready. I sat on a cut-off stump for maybe twenty minutes. Then, a flash of brown caught my eye as the buck closed in on me. He was no more than fifty yards away, just loping along broadside at a run. I pulled my .30-.30 up and took careful aim.

The shot, of course, missed. I was working that lever-action rifle like I saw the Rifleman do it on the TV show. So I loaded another round and took another shot. But, damn it, I missed him again. I had time to load one more time, but he'd gotten into heavy cover. It was over.

In a few minutes, Joe came along. "Well, where's he at?" he asked.

"Could be in Warrens now for all I know."

"I saw him ahead of me, and he looked pretty nice. How many points do you think he had?

"He had twelve points."

"Are you sure you missed it?"

"I couldn't find any blood on the ground, but we can look again if you want."

"Sure, why don't we do that as we go to the car? This woodlot is too small to hunt all day. I'd like to try north of Aunt Margret's place."

We slowly surveyed the terrain to see if I'd missed something. Finally, we decided the buck probably would have stayed in the heavy cover. A ribbon of small pine trees ran toward the car. "Do you think he'd follow these pines to the driveway?" I asked Joe.

"Sure he would have. Let's take it back to the car."

We jumped four does just before the driveway with a couple of half-grown fawns. They lay not more than seventy-five yards from the car. They were just lying around, getting their beauty sleep, while I was making a fool of myself again.

They cleared the driveway and ran to where Joe had entered the woods. I wondered, "Joe, do you think the buck did the same thing as this doe? You know I could try to jump him out to you. But on the other hand, he might have just made a big circle."

"No, let's go. The buck is long gone." To this day, I wonder if we would have spent more time hunting him we would've gotten the big boy. I was halfway there, hunting like a lion but shooting like a blueberry picker.

We grabbed a sandwich and a cup of coffee when we returned to the trailer. A six-point was hanging, so someone connected this morning. We were halfway to the highway when dad and the rest of the gang pulled up. Dad said, "We are going to make a few drives."

"Oh, goody," I said. I just hated the hell out of driving deer. But, of course, I wasn't in charge. We put the best shots on the stands; guys like me were the dogs. That was right. Why go to all the effort if you can't produce something?

We drove the highland swamp to a marsh grass opening. We were close to the end of the drive when the shooting started. Several does ran back through the drive, and Joe shot a four-point. That's what I hated about drives. It got dangerous with both standers and drivers shooting.

An eight-pointer had gone out at the end of the drive. We checked and had blood, so we waited a few minutes to track the buck. The buck had just crossed the road and was dead hanging on a barbed-wire fence a few hundred yards up.

We tried one more drive. This time all the deer came back through the drive. The piece we drove was too big to cover, and we got nothing. Good, we could quit driving and hang up these bucks.

The guys had to return to Racine to work the next day, so I cleaned up things a little and went to stay with Uncle Hipe and Aunt Margret for the rest of the season.

Hipe told his tales of living in the logging camps during his working years. He brought out a flat stone and began to sharpen his hunting knife. He stuck out his arm and shaved the hair off.

"Is that sharp enough?" I asked.

"I need it sharp, I'm going to get a buck tomorrow," Hipe replied.

We hunted together in the hills on Monday and saw a few tails. He was wrong about getting one tomorrow. Late on that day, it started to snow hard. By ten o'clock, we had a good four inches on the ground. We knew the deer would move into the heavy cover of the swamps.

The following day we hunted until noon with no luck. Finally, we came in for lunch. Aunt Margret fried some fresh venison loins for us. We'd split the party doe up four ways. She was waiting to see what else we got before getting out a canner.

Warm biscuits and American fries accompanied the venison. We finished a couple of cups of coffee and made plans for the afternoon hunt. I was to circle north across the creek in the highland swamp and kick the area where Hipe had cut wood that fall.

The sun was out, and the snow was dropping off the trees. There was constant noise to cover my approach. The snow was wet, so I made very little noise. We always checked the wind direction. It takes very little wind for your scent to be picked up by deer. The weather made it a perfect afternoon for jump hunting.

Hipe had logged off a strip of woods a couple of years prior. The small brush had started to come up, and there were lots of stumps to sit on. He knew in this weather, with snow on the ground, that's where they'd travel.

I slowly stalked the brush piles of oak trees. I'd walked a few yards and stopped to watch ahead, then I repeated the stalk, working my way slowly toward Hipe's hiding place. It was beautiful in the woods with the sun glistening off the new snow. I saw the woods like the Native Americans had seen them a thousand years ago.

I could see deer legs in the thick cover ahead but not the body. I aimed my rifle but could not get a shot at the deer. When I raised the gun to shoot, the deer seemed to disappear. I didn't have a doe permit, so I had to ensure it was a buck.

I froze for a few minutes, watching for movement in the thick cover. Then, something moved close to me from the corner of my eye. A great-horned owl slowly turned his head around to look at me. Then, it took flight, and the commotion startled the deer. Dang it, I'd been busted by an owl. How unlucky can a guy get? After all this great stalking, at the last minute, an owl decided to mess up my hunt.

The legs turned into a spike buck on the run, with another following him. They came out of the cover at a pretty good clip. I had only a few seconds for a shot and decided not to take one. I think I could have connected. Unfortunately, the shot would have been right up the rear, spoiling the hindquarters.

I started to count: *one thousand one, one thousand two, one thousand three, one thousand four.* I got to one thousand ten before I heard Hipe shoot. Just one shot, hm. I thought he'd shoot both of them.

After a few minutes, I tracked the deer to where Hipe had ambushed the small buck. "Did you shoot both of them with one shot?" I asked.

"Na, was the other one a buck too? He came a little too far for me to get a shot."

"Yep, it looked just like this one."

"Speaking of looks, take a look at the pretty boy."

I could not believe my eyes. The buck had white rings around both eyes. No other marking was out of the norm for deer. "Have you ever seen markings like that before?"

"No, never. I've seen them with spots and even an all-white one once, but never one marked like this."

"Well, we will just have to call him pretty boy, won't we?"

We laughed, and I kidded him about shooting a buck with such beautiful eyes. He field dressed him with that sharp knife in no time. I pulled him to the road while Hipe carried the guns. There was a fire lane, so the pulling was easy on the fresh snow.

He walked to the house to get his Rambler, one of the cars my dad probably put together. Unfortunately, they were terrible cars that the front wheels would fall off of while driving them. When he returned, we loaded the buck onto a tarp he had placed in the trunk. We left the head hanging out. The game warden wanted to see the deer's head in those days.

You had to metal tag the deer and make sure the tag snapped closed. It seemed to me the DNR was overly protective of the resource, which made no sense. Most country folks shot the deer they wanted to eat in September.

So we started for home, and I remember singing a song about his Rambler. It went like this: "When you're riding in your Rambler, the whole world laughs at you."

Hipe replied, "It beats walking, doesn't it?"

"Not by much."

"Keep singing, and you'll find out how much it beats walking."

We hung the buck and removed the heart and lungs. We saved the heart and liver for pickling or frying with onions. Aunt Margret had supper ready. We washed up from the gut job, sat for supper, and enjoyed a fine meal of mashed potatoes, pork chops, sweet peas, and biscuits. I helped her do dishes while we talked of days gone by.

Her dad and mother had this place when it was a log house. Her second husband had covered the logs with siding and built in this kitchen. She'd been in this place all her life. Living a simple life, she had very little need for the world rushing by at the speed of a bullet.

There was a hand pump just outside the kitchen that still worked. The family used it in emergencies if the electricity went out. They heated and cooked on two wood stoves, one in the kitchen and the other in the living room.

She hung her clothes outside on a clothesline. They'd freeze harder than a rock, and she'd bring them into the house to finish drying on a rack by the fire.

A massive woodpile of oak was put up for the winter behind the house. Hipe always cut wood; matter of fact, he died of a heart attack at seventy-nine after cutting wood.

He didn't even go to the doctor for it. He went to bed and died at home. He told Aunt Margret if he didn't feel better by morning, he'd go to the doctor.

They had an outhouse and used it in good weather.

The garden was about an acre, with every vegetable you could imagine planted in it. He worked it mainly with a hand hoe. He even raised popcorn. They also belonged to the land, like the wild things in the woods.

We were done with supper dishes, and it was time for conversation around the woodstove in the living room. They had a couple of rocking chairs that creaked as they rocked. Hipe would smoke a cigarette or grab a finger of snuff. Offer me a finger. "No, thanks." I couldn't stand the stuff.

He then relived the day's events, committing this buck to his memory of the hunt. He asked Margret, "Do you have enough canning lids to process this pretty boy?"

"Sure I do. The buck is pretty, but not pretty big," Margret said with a smile.

Hipe replied, "You see what I have to put up with?"

The fire crackled, and the conversation continued until Hipe tired. It had been a perfect day in a hunter's life. The meat pole had a nice buck hanging for processing. Both of us took this buck. We used the weather conditions and our knowledge of the woods to outsmart the buck.

I did not shoot my buck that year. That would come in the next year's hunt. Hipe put the hammer down on the pretty boy. Of course, that wouldn't have happened without me jumping the buck to him. We were lions, complimenting each other's abilities.

My understanding of the wild was growing. This year I learned that deer rely on birds and other animals to warn them of danger. There are different songs in the woods that creatures of the wild hear. If one sits quietly, you can listen in on them.

It might start with the ruffle of leaves as a gray squirrel forages for acorns. Chickadees may come in the next movement as they fly from branch to branch. Next, you might hear woodpeckers drilling holes in trees for insects. It's genuinely a composition of music created by Mother Nature.

I wondered whether I could be the Wolfgang Amadeus Mozart of the forest. It wasn't as simple as understanding each note. It was the entire composition one needed to understand.

When the owl flew out of that tree, I could not hear his wings flap, but the deer did. Sounds, smells, or movements will give away my presence in the forest. I'd have to learn to be more careful.

3

FIRST BUCK

For almost six months, I'd had my eye on a 30.06 Remington semi-automatic rifle down at the local gun shop. My friend Bill and I would check on it every few weeks. The guy who owned the store was named Red. He and his old buddies would sit around a wooden barrel playing dirty clubs most afternoons. When we came in, Red never even stopped playing cards.

The rifle was new, with a price of $110 on it. One day I was admiring the gun. Red said, "If you can get ninety dollars together, I will sell it to you."

I thought about it for a couple of seconds and said, "I'll take it. Can you hold it for two weeks for me? I'm working pulling onions for Horner's Onion Farm. I should have enough money by then."

"OK, I need a little money to hold it. Do you have ten dollars?"

"Well, sure I do," I said, sounding like that was chump change. Fortunately, I had twelve dollars in my wallet.

"I'll write it up for you. Just let me finish beating

these losers in cards." Cards were more important than selling guns. I think he just ran the store to have enough money for cards. As they finished their game, Red swore, "You goddamn boys must be cheating." They all laughed.

One of the players remarked, "Playing with Red is like stealing candy from a baby."

Another player said, "He's winning, or he's whining with his pants full of shit." More laughter and swearing.

Red rose from the barrel, looking for something. After a few minutes of rummaging around, he found his receipt pads. He took my money, giving me a receipt for the down payment.

I walked out of that store with my head high, feeling like I had made the deal of a lifetime. Just two more weeks of working in the hot fields, pulling onions, and I would own a 30.06.

Ninety dollars was a considerable amount of money for me to come by. I mowed lawns, shoveled snow, picked strawberries, and pulled onions. It took me six months to save enough for my first new gun. I also sold my .30-.30 Winchester for thirty-five dollars to have enough money to complete the deal.

When I went to pick it up, Red asked, "Do you have a case for it?

"No, I don't. Will that be extra?"

"I should charge you, but I got a good deal on those on the bottom shelf. Pick out one; I'll throw it in with the deal."

"Thanks. What grain of shells should I use for

hunting in heavy cover, maybe shooting a hundred fifty yards at the most?"

"The guys tell me they like the one eighty grain best for all-around shooting, so they start at a hundred and fifty grains and run to two hundred and twenty grains. Whatever you decide, stick to it after you get your gun lined up."

"Got a sling for it?"

"Oh, you bet I do." He reached under the counter, pulling out a beautiful leather sling.

"That looks darn expensive. How much is it?"

"It's six bucks, and I'll mount it for you."

I checked my wallet. I did have enough money for everything. "OK, I'll take it."

It took about fifteen minutes for him to mount it. When he finished, he bore sighted the rifle. He said, "It's right on, young fellow. You know, the boys like venison sausage if you have an extra chunk laying around after the hunt."

"If Dad decides to get some made, I'll drop you off a chunk." I cased the gun and proudly walked the five miles home.

Being poor was a blessing. Hard work came along with my wants. Red knew how hard it was for me to save the money for that rifle. I mattered to him. In later years, I'd see him at the Eagles Club on Friday nights. Can you believe Lake Michigan perch was ninety cents a plate? He asked, "Do you still have the 30.06 I sold you?"

I answered, "You bet. I took my first buck with it."

The gun was almost ready for the fall hunt. The only thing left was checking the sites to see if they were on. So Dad took us out sometime each September to try out the guns. A family friend had cut the stock off and installed a stock pad for me. It fit me like a glove, even with a heavy coat.

It was a Sunday, so Dad had off work. We tried the guns out in an abandoned sandpit. I was a little apprehensive about how much the rifle would kick. When I took my first shot, I pulled the trigger too hard, causing the gun to shoot left on the bull's-eye four inches. Opening jitters were the problem. After all, the gun didn't kick any harder than the .30-.30. In the next three shots, I formed a half-inch pattern just off the bull's-eye.

We hunted pheasants along a drainage ditch before going home. We got three roosters and a rabbit. Unfortunately, the dog jumped a muskrat and got bit in the face before killing it. As a result, the dog bled all over Dad's car on the way home. Dad strung together a half dozen swear words to reprimand me for the mess. When we got home, I pulled the stick tights off him and cleaned up the bites with peroxide.

Deer hunting rolled around, and once again, the opener was here. I decided to hunt with Hipe and Deep on an opening day. We hunted the hills to the east of the farm. Again, it was a warm opener, with no snow on the ground.

After parking the car in a fire lane, we walked down the fire lane for a few hundred yards. Ahead of us, two deer bounded off, showing their whitetails. Hipe said, "That one is a buck for sure."

"How do you know that?"

"He has a small tail with a good-size body. Tell you what, I'll circle and put them back to you when I return. You sit on this hillside." He pointed to the hill that ran off to the south.

"Now, don't you get in a hurry. It might take me a few hours."

"OK, I got it."

He took Deep with him and placed him on another hill adjacent to me. I found a good hiding place about three-quarters of the way up the hill. An old hollow oak had fallen in a windstorm, making a perfect hide for me.

I sat there for at least two and a half hours. I'd just pulled out my stash of hard candy. I was searching for the right piece when I heard something coming from the oak leaves. I readied the new 30.06 for a shot. A set of deer horns appeared just over the horizon of the ridge. Then the rest of the body came into sight.

It was a nice nine-pointer just walking broadside. The buck came within seventy-five yards and stopped. When I pulled the trigger, the buck fell on his front knees. Then just as quickly, he got back up and ran over the hill.

My heart was pumping, and I sprang to my feet. I hurried over to the spot where I had taken the shot. Blood, and lots of it, was on the ground. Oh boy, I got this one for sure. In my excitement, I broke one of the basic rules of hunting. I should have waited fifteen minutes before tracking him.

Over the hill I went, hoping to see the buck lying. He had run to the first heavy cover and lay down. I came along, watching the blood trail too closely, and jumped him back up. When I saw him, he was going out of sight.

I tracked him to the road we'd come in on. There was blood, and I found pieces of flesh on sticks along the way. I had just walked across the road when I heard a shot ahead of me.

Another hunter shot the buck a few hundred yards from me. When I got there, two hunters were standing over the buck. That buck was mine, I told them. They thought the buck wasn't hit that bad, and it belonged to them. I said that the buck was hit plenty hard and was about to die from blood loss.

I said, "You two bastards, my uncle had done the work of jumping him to me. You're horning in on our hunt." That only made things worse. One of them pushed me and called me a little asshole. They threatened to knock the shit out of me.

"You fucker, I'm going to get my uncle," I said, and steamed off. I gave them the finger and told them I'd be back with my uncle. Uncle Hipe and Deep were sitting in the car when I returned. I told them what had happened, and Hipe said, "We'll see about this."

I knew where they'd parked their car. When we got there, the car was gone. You could see where they'd pulled the buck out. They must have loaded the buck without even gutting it. It was a lesson for me. Hipe had done all the work for this buck, and I screwed it up by chasing the buck to these assholes.

I should have taken down their back tag numbers or license plate. If Uncle Hipe had caught them, they would have been going home without that buck, or to the hospital.

After supper, Hipe and I talked about the whole thing. I remember saying, "I should have stayed and taken them on over the buck."

Hipe asked, "What if it got out of hand and someone got shot?"

"Na, I wouldn't go that far. I'm talking black eyes and bloody noses. I don't plan on ever shooting anyone over a buck. Still, I wouldn't mind kicking them in the balls."

I could tell Hipe was checking to see if he had to give me a session of homespun counseling. "Good, but it can get out of hand when guns are involved."

"Don't worry. I can control my temper. I learned it from having Jim as an older brother. Every scar on his body came from me."

"So?" Uncle Hipe said, questioning.

"Well, I never shot him, did I?"

We both laughed. "Don't get me wrong, I won't mind making their old acorns sore myself."

It turned out Hipe was right. I would kill men for less reason than a trophy buck a few years later. When guns are present, things do get out of hand. The Vietnam War would make killers out of many young men my age.

At times, even a lion does not get to eat his kill. A

couple of blueberry pickers will steal it from him. But it was my fault for chasing the buck. He was down and hit plenty hard. I just had to let him die.

Deep never shot a deer in all the years he hunted with us. I think he just came along because he liked the guys in the hunting party. He was a great cook, and as I said, his stories were interesting. I believe the buck must have traveled very close to him. Then, of course, it was a lovely day for a nap, which old Deep would take occasionally.

The party had taken a few bucks on the opener. We were planning the next day's hunt when Joe popped up with the idea of hunting Aunt Annie's place. Brother Joe and Floyd both came along with me the following day.

Annie had inherited six hundred acres above Warrens. I remember, Annie always had white hair and a light complexion. A fine-featured woman, walking with a graceful gait, she wore only cotton dresses with sensible footwear.

If you visited her, she'd take you to the garden for inspection, then prepare a meal for you to eat and send you home with vegetables from the garden.

Her son Norbert started a cranberry marsh on the site. He never married and, except for a tour of duty in the army, lived at home all his life. He was a very gentle man.

One day he butchered a pig, and the rest of the pigs put up a fuss. It made him so upset he never butchered a pig again. He'd become attached to the pigs and didn't realize it until that day.

Right after that, he bought a nice-looking collie dog. It fulfilled his need to connect with a pet. A skunk got into the back porch and bit Aunt Annie before the dog killed it.

Sure enough, the skunk had rabies. Aunt Annie had to endure painful shots in her stomach, and the poor dog was put down. Norbert did get another dog, but he had a hard time with losing his dog.

Grandfather was a wise old Irishman who'd accumulated a lot of wealth by buying property during the Depression. On the other hand, my dad's family accumulated nothing. They all worked hard but didn't know what to do with their money.

I was a product of two families, one pretty darn smart, the other dumber than hell. Oh, Lord, it's hard to be humble.

We arrived early on Sunday morning and hunted around the marsh for a few hours. My cousin Norbert spotted us. He mentioned, "You guys should try back at the house. The deer have been feeding on the acorns lately."

It was high ground with oaks and a few pine trees—the typical above Warrens' sandy soil, where the trees never got huge. The soil was so poor, the crows had to pack a lunch to fly across a forty.

We spread out, taking the woods around to a narrow ribbon of pine trees. I found a stump to sit on and watched for deer. A three-point buck appeared, running not fifty yards from me, and stopped. I raised my new 30.06 and put the front bead on his shoulder, just behind the leg.

Boom! The gun went off. The buck took off running in an unnatural pattern. I could tell I had a good shot at him. I had learned my lesson from the nine-point buck, so I held still. I observed where he'd run and clicked the safety back on while glancing at my watch. It was ten forty-five. I'd sit there until eleven before I stirred. After about ten minutes, Joe showed up.

"What did you get? It sounded like you connected with something."

"He's got three points, and I don't think he'll go far." From where Joe was standing, he could see the blood trail.

"You've got plenty of blood. The buck is dead, for sure. Let's look. Keep your gun ready."

"Well, if the buck is dead, why am I keeping my gun ready?"

We slowly followed the blood trail, Joe watching the blood and me watching ahead for movement. We hadn't gone one hundred fifty yards, and there he lay. Finally, I'd taken my first buck. Well, we'd all taken him. One of my brothers had kicked him out.

I was a happy kid. Not the nine-point buck, but my first to hang on the meat pole. I'd placed the shot correctly for a good, clean kill. I'd waited until he died before tracking him down. All that was left to do was gut him and pull him to the road. We were back at the trailer, hanging him on the meat pole within an hour.

It sounds silly now to have put so much importance on a deer hunt. But I guess with four brothers and Dad prodding, deer hunting took on a larger-than-life importance. I'd shown them I could piss as high as they could on the bushes.

The weather turned brutally cold for the Thanksgiving Day weekend. I was helping my brother Jim hunt. We had gone to some woods we'd never hunted before. It was up along Hableman's cranberry marsh.

The terrain had a lot of downed trees. The trees had such shallow root systems that the wind would blow them over when they got tall. It was wet in the marsh much of the year. The big freeze had stiffened up the ground, allowing us access to hunt.

As we got into the marsh, you could see deep trails where the deer had traveled. We stayed on the trail as much as possible because if you wandered off it, you sounded like a herd of buffalo coming through the woods.

We hadn't gone far when we put up a couple of deer. They ran into a thick pine island. "What do you think, Jim? Want me to make a circle and push them to you?"

"Sure, let me back out of here a little and set up a stand."

The weather being that cold, I'm glad I didn't have to stand. I hurried along, knowing Jim could only stand for a short period. I'd circle to the other side of the island and penetrate the thick pine. I could hear the deer going out the other side of the pine.

Boom! Boom! Jim had taken a couple of shots. I stood

there for a few minutes to catch my breath. Then, I heard another round of shots. I waited, thinking maybe something would come my way. Finally, after a few minutes, I started to walk toward the noise.

When I cleared the thick pine, a five-point buck was pulling himself toward me. Jim had shot it high in the back and paralyzed the buck's back legs. I pulled up and shot the buck in the neck. He went down, and Jim was there within a few minutes.

He'd hit the buck with the first shot, and all the rest of the booming was Jim trying for a killing shot. His gun, a 30.06 semi-automatic, had jammed. Those guns were good for that, especially in cold conditions. It had taken him that long to unjam the weapon.

He was sweating like a pig, all worked up from chasing after the buck. Now, how were we going to get this boy out of here? It was close to dark, so we did a quick gut job. I had brought along a dragging rope. We put that rope around the buck's horns and began to pull.

The ordeal was unbelievably harrowing. The buck kept getting stuck in the bog. So, we pulled hard, and suddenly, the buck lunged forward. That caused us to lose our balance and fall.

We took turns pulling on him, and we felt like we'd gone a few rounds with King Kong when we reached the road. I looked at Jim. "Next time you wound one, drive him toward the car."

We laughed and waited to catch our breath before loading the buck. Darkness had set in, and the wind was picking up. Usually, the wind goes down around dusk, so we knew a storm was coming.

It snowed that night like a December snowstorm. There were big drifts of snow outside the trailer the following day. The temperatures were freezing. The buck was stiff as a board when we took him down from the meat pole.

That ended the hunt for that year. We loaded up the buck and headed for home. It took us five hours to get home, usually a three-hour trip in good weather. The good thing about the cold was that the meat would keep for a few days.

We waited three days before skinning the deer. That was a big mistake, and the hide was frozen. It was a bear to get off. We had to thaw the meat a little before cutting it up. The process was much more challenging because of the cold. Finally, we salted and rolled the hides up.

All that was left to do was sell the hides. Dad decided he wanted a buckskin jacket. We had enough hides to make one. Dad sent them to a tannery, and they delivered a beautiful coat within six weeks. We also received four pairs of gloves.

My first buck, indeed this was a fantastic year for me. Brother Jim scored a kill. That might have been his second buck. Finally, it was time to enter our rightful place in the hunting party.

4

FLOYD'S STALK

I was hunting with my brother Floyd and my brother-in-law Jim Kline a couple of miles west of Aunt Margret's farm. I remember there wasn't any snow. The woods we hunted were mostly oak trees. I could hear squirrels feeding as soon as the sun rose.

I sat overlooking a valley with open timber. Saw a deer come through around eight o'clock. I swear it was a buck, but I was sure there were no horns. Then, I heard something behind me. I thought it was those pesky squirrels, so I didn't turn around.

In a few minutes, I heard the snort of a deer. I jerked the gun up and turned around. A buck was going back over the crest of the hill. Oh well, another mistake to add to my list.

About forty-five minutes had passed, and a herd of deer were coming up the valley I was watching. There were about ten of them. They were all does and fawns with their tongues hanging out. They were so tired from running that when they saw me, they just walked over the hill.

I heard a shot across the road. I knew these does hadn't gotten that far yet. So I watched closely, picking up a lone deer from the hillside. Right away, I spotted the buck's rack. It didn't appear that the buck would stop, so I readied the gun for a running shot.

There was a thin growth of pine trees in the valley. When the buck cleared the last one, I took good aim. *Boom!* The buck reversed his direction and retreated to where he'd come from. I didn't see him go up the other hill, and I wondered if he'd stop down in the pines. I sat quietly, watching for movement. Behind me, I heard more noise. This time, I turned to see Jim, my brother-in-law.

I put my finger to my mouth to silence him.

"What you get?" he whispered.

"I think I've got a buck down." I motioned for him to sit, and he did. We watched the area for at least ten minutes before moving.

We climbed to the top of the hill. We strolled down a fire lane to where I'd last seen the buck. Right after we cleared the pines, I could see him lying. No movement, but we advanced carefully. We didn't want to flush him.

As we closed in on him, I saw he wasn't going any-where, so we relaxed and went to take a look at him. He had seven points on not a big rack. Probably weighed one-forty, give or take. I'd made a good shot, hitting him right in the heart, running.

Now, how were we going to get this boy to the top of the hill? I pulled his head toward the steep hillside to gut him out. Jim took the guns to the hilltop and brought a rope back. We both had to pull and then hold him so he didn't slide back down the hill. It was hard work to reach the top.

Once we were at the top, we rested before returning to our stands. I'd stood for less than an hour before I saw movement below me. Sure enough, it was a four-point buck standing in heavy cover. Something seemed wrong with the way he'd come in.

I gave him an excellent leaning shot, and down he went. He never moved from where he stood. I could see he was dead, so I climbed down the hill after him. The buck had an injury in the front quarter. A car must have broken its front leg.

I carefully gutted him out. I was checking for any signs of rotten meat. He looked all right, with no smell of spoilage. He appeared to be OK, so I called Jim to tag him.

We did our rope trick again to the top of the hill. Just as we cleared the top of the hill, Floyd came along. He had missed his buck and was in a foul mood. He wanted to call it a day. We loaded the bucks and headed for the trailer. A six-point that Dad had shot was hanging when we got there.

I finally found the trick to shooting them on the run. In my early years of hunting, I was trying to hit the bull's-eye on a running deer just behind the front leg. Of course, that's the ideal shot, but it is easier to aim for a barrel top.

I noticed that neither Dad's nor Uncle Hipe's deer were perfect shots right through the heart every time.

Many times they had to shoot them a couple of times. The shots were always in the front of the deer, maybe in the neck or front shoulders. I was trying to take too fine a bead that would cause me to shoot behind the deer.

I imagine a sharpshooter would tell you that I'm wrong. I should have been able to place a shot by pulling the trigger without hesitation. That may be true in theory, but not in the real world of my hunting experience. However, in my later years of hunting, I did become more efficient in following a running target.

I had a buddy named Dan Derosia, a gunner on a helicopter in Vietnam. He was the best shot I've ever known. He told me stories of shooting the Charlie on the run. (Charlie was a name I called the enemy in Vietnam.)

The Charlie were running, and the choppers were also moving. We shot in a trap together, and Dan always did better than me. I never hunted deer with him. He hunted way up north with his dad. Anyway, he had a peep sight on his gun, which wasn't for target shooting. It was barrel-top shooting.

On the second day, my uncle Charlie showed up. He wanted us to help him get a deer, which meant we'd be driving deer. Have I told you I hated that?

Charlie was Dad's younger brother. Charlie and his wife, Dorothy, were alcoholics all their lives. They'd come to the house drunk. First, they'd get into a fight, then Dorothy would slap Charlie in the face. I remember one time when they had shown up drunk and were standing in the front yard talking. An old hound we had lifted his leg and pissed on Dorothy. We all laughed, and she insisted we shoot the dog. Dad refused. She stormed off, calling my dad a son of a bitch. She sat in the car until they left. I always wondered how long it took Dad to teach the old hound that trick.

Charlie drove a truck for a living and never drank while on the road. Well, when he got home, they made up for it. Thank God they never had children. They always drove expensive cars and showed up to show off their wealth to a struggling farm family.

But where was I? We were to drive the swamp to a dirt road you could shoot off. Uncle Charlie, Dad, and my brother Joe were standers. We were dropped off about a mile from the stands.

When we got to the end of the drive, the shooting started. There must have been ten shots from a couple of different guns. Dad must have talked Joe into taking his .35 Remington Woodsmaster. I heard it booming on the roadway. Then I heard Charlie screaming, "They're going back through the drive."

I got ready, thinking something was going to run me over. A doe came within twenty yards and circled me. I could see the doe had been gutshot. The doe stopped, not able to go any further. This had to be Charlie's doing, I thought, so I shot her to end her suffering.

Charlie came rushing from the front of the drive. He was all out of breath and screaming. "Did you get him? Did you get him?"

"Sure did, and he is a she."

"Oh, that's all right; I've got a doe tag."

"Good, then you've got some meat."

I was glad to help him gut the doe. After that, he was no longer interested in hunting. We loaded the doe, and off he drove. I guess Dad put up with him because he was family. He wasn't a hunter for sure and dangerous to be around in the woods. If a deer came through, he'd shoot until he was out of shells.

Joe picked me up on the blacktop road. He'd shot an eight-pointer full of holes. There wasn't going to be much meat from that deer. So we returned to the trailer and hung him on the meal pole.

This following story was told to me by my older brother Floyd. I wasn't on this hunt with him, but he is a gifted storyteller. I hope I get this right.

He lived south of town, just this side of the hill country that runs to the Mississippi River. As I told you, we'd hunted together for the opener. It was Monday, and light snow had fallen early, around four o'clock in the morning. There was less than two inches of fresh snow on the ground.

He wanted to do a walkabout from his place. In the farm country south of town, the woods are small. They run along hillsides too steep to plow. However, pine trees were planted just across from his house. The plantation of pines was only a couple of acres, but the deer would hole up in the pines in snowy weather.

He started his hunt in the pine trees. He came in downwind, watching for any signs of movement. Nothing flushed but a covey of pigeons and a red fox. He was almost through when he picked up a set of deer tracks.

They, of course, were fresh and looked to be from a good-size deer.

The deer had gone out across a cow pasture that turned into small wetlands with high grass. Unfortunately, Floyd lost track in the tall grasses of the wetlands. He guessed where he thought the deer would have gone into the woods, surveying the fence line that separated the woodlot from the field. Sure enough, he picked up the tracks on his second trip along the fence line.

The deer had traveled in a shallow valley concealed from the county road. The valley slowly rose to the top of a hill that ran like horseshoes around an old sand pit. There were stands of poison sumac with a backdrop of white birch trees. Any one of these groves of sumac could be a hiding place.

He explored each hiding place, aware of the wind and coming in quiet. Then, the tracks seemed to have suddenly ended. There was nothing ahead of him but a blank canvas of snow. He checked again and again to see what had happened. Then, finally, he noticed a footprint coming back at him. The deer had backtracked down the same path it had gone up on.

Taking the trail back about fifty yards, he picked up where the deer had veered off the path. He continued to track the deer over another hill. By this time, he'd been stalking that deer for two hours. He'd walked over three miles from home. Finally, the woods were ending. All that was left was a ditch that ran out into a field.

At this point, he wondered if the deer had crossed

a large hayfield to another woodlot. The hay was long and could have easily concealed the deer tracks. The spirits of our family's hunting ancestors spoke to him. "Floyd, check the ditch." He noticed the ditch had a small brush thicket halfway down. He wondered if that deer was holing up in that cover.

Again, the spirits spoke. "After all this effort, it wouldn't hurt you to take the ditch to the road, would it?"

"You're right; I'll give it a try."

About one hundred yards down, he stopped to rest. When he did, an eight-point buck flushed from the small brush thicket. Startled by the buck, Floyd's first shot missed. Then, the buck turned and gave him a broadside shot. This shot found its target, and the buck dropped. He was dead before Floyd closed the distance between them.

The buck had lived in farm country and learned that the safest place to hole up was in the open. I'm sure hunters had hunted the wooded land all weekend. The buck only needed a few small brushes to conceal his hiding place. Those old bucks were old because they'd developed strategies to hide their presence. It takes an old hunter to hang an old buck on the meat pole.

The weather had given Floyd a perfect setup for a stalk. So, during the early hours of the morning, the buck may have gone on his walkabout. But on the other hand, he may have still been in the rut, out looking to bash heads with the smaller bucks in the area.

Of course, Floyd could have also pushed him from the pines. The old buck might have just stayed far enough ahead of him to be out of sight.

He looked like the boss in that area to me. He had a nice set of horns in a good weight class. The buck looked better than a lot of bucks after the rutting season. Probably around four to five years old. It's hard to guess the age of deer.

Bucks in farm country with excellent feed look better than the bucks shot in sand country. The only way to tell their age is to look at their teeth.

Floyd was three miles from home and didn't want to pull the buck that far. He gutted the buck and pulled him close to the road, then concealed the buck from the view of the hyenas that prowled the roadways. He started walking down the road toward home.

He hadn't gotten far when a farmer stopped his pickup truck and offered a ride. He was taking feed to the mill for grinding for the cattle. He milked cows and fattened a few steers for the market. He saw Floyd had blood on his hands.

"Did you get one?"

"Yep, shot a nice eight-pointer down in that ditch."

"Well, drag him up here. I want to take a look at him."

"OK, I'll be right back." Floyd pulled the buck to the truck, and the guy got out and helped load the buck on top of the feed sacks.

"Congratulations, nice buck you got there."

"Yep, it took me all morning to track him down."

"Did you see anything else?"

"No, he was the only one in those woods for three miles."

"That doesn't surprise me. I have two hundred acres of land with less than a half dozen deer on it."

This old farmer took him to his place and helped him unload the buck. The farmers in that area might get out a little over the hunting season but weren't that serious about hunting. They had to milk cows before the milk truck showed up.

On a farm, work comes first; there are no days off. They indeed weren't worried about venison when they had all the best beef in the world to eat.

They also didn't believe that the deer belonged to them. Farmers had little use for wooded land that came along with the farm. Sometimes they pastured it if they figured the value of the feed was worth the fencing cost.

Farmers were family people who cared about the people that lived in the community, like this old farmer who took time out of his day to help Floyd get his buck home.

After Thanksgiving, we decided to skin and cut up the deer. When we got to the four-point buck I shot the first day, the meat was all green on one side of him. He'd been suffering for some time; the meat was spoiled. So we discarded the entire deer. Oh well, we had plenty of meat. Glad I put him down. I just wished we'd investigated more before we took him home.

This hunt was a year for Floyd to remember. He is now in his early eighties and still can tell that story of the day when he outsmarted a trophy buck—remembering a time when hunting made sense—when the lions took deer, not the hyenas or blueberry pickers.

5

MIKE AND CHUCK SHOOT THEIR FIRST BUCKS

Growing up, my wife, Shi, lived in Union Grove, Wisconsin. Her next-door neighbor's name was Cheryl Alby. Cheryl married a Vietnam veteran named Mike Theigs. After returning from Vietnam, Mike and I became good friends.

He grew up without a father to introduce him to hunting. After purchasing all the hunting gear, he decided to join our gang. Like all hunters, it took Mike a few years to figure out the sport.

This particular year we decided to hunt on conservation land east of Warrens. Private land was becoming harder and harder to get on. It was low land with scrub oak and small pine trees. The piece was only a few miles square, so you didn't have to worry about getting lost. We had gotten in early to set up on our stands. I remember it was cold until the sun came up. Just before light, I saw a deer go through that looked like a buck. It was too early to shoot, so I let it go. Then right after,

I heard someone open up on the deer a few hundred yards from me.

Interesting, I thought. I heard a couple of guys talking around seven, and a few minutes later, a guy pulled a small buck by me.

"When did you get him? I asked.

"Just shot him."

"Did you shoot him with an arrow?"

"No, I shot him with a gun."

We both knew he'd shot him before the season had opened. I didn't care if he had taken the buck too early. I just wondered how he knew how many hunters may have been in his shooting lane. It's hard to see orange after dark.

I took a little walkabout to see what the rest of the swamp looked like. I walked a while before finding a natural hiding place. I slowly worked my way close to a fire lane. I sat down, leaned back on a rotten stump, and got comfortable.

I heard shooting from across the road and readied my gun for a shot at a buck. But instead, a doe came bounding right in front of me. The doe stopped, stomped her front leg, and then snorted before circling me. I watched her as she disappeared into the small pines.

Something told me to look behind me. So I did, and there stood a small fork buck. The buck also stomped his front leg and snorted. I was thinking, *How can I turn around to get a shot at this buck?* I hadn't gotten that processed before the buck took off.

He ran in such a pattern that I could not get a bead on him. Sometimes they can be close, but you still can't shoot them. That was the case with him, and I never got a shot. Dang it! In about fifteen minutes, Mike came wandering along. I got up to chew the fat with him. Then, we heard shooting across the road from us. "Get ready, Mike." We both watched ahead for any movement.

In a few minutes, a couple of does came through. A six-point buck followed them in and stopped not more than fifty yards away. We both pulled up to shoot, Mike shot, and the buck went down. That was his first buck. He was rightfully very proud of himself. We gutted the buck out and pulled him to the road.

After taking his first buck, Mike was officially hooked on deer hunting. The following year his father-in-law, Chuck Alby, came along for the hunt. Chuck was a huge man with a great sense of humor. He'd tell a story and then laugh at himself.

We had taken a few bucks on the opening day. It was Sunday, and we hunted over on an abandoned farm north of Tunnel City. The plan was for Floyd and Norbert, my little brother, to push a narrow piece.

I stood with my brother Jim watching a hayfield just in case they broke out the side of the drive. Mike and Chuck stood at the end of the drive where we thought they would go out.

Floyd and Norbert took the hayfield down to a fence line about a quarter mile to the east. They cut into a narrow valley with many crabapple trees growing in it.

They were about halfway back when an eight-point and a fork buck broke out the side of the drive.

Jim, my brother, shot first, flipping the eight-point buck over. Then, the fork buck ran back to the woods, and I shot him. He didn't go down, but I could tell I had a good shot at him. Meanwhile, the eight-point got back up and also ran for the woods.

The fork buck kept going, crossing the road just in front of Chuck. After crossing, he just lay down in some small brush. Chuck screamed at me, "What should I do?"

I knew the buck was done for it, but I told him to shoot it in the neck. So he walked up to within twenty feet of the buck and plugged him in the neck. "Nice shot, Chuck. You got your buck."

A big smile came across his face, and Mike grabbed the buck's horns to pull him onto the road. I turned when Jim opened up on the eight-point. He was about to run down over a pile of tin cans and old tires. I motioned for him to stop, but he just kept on going.

That was a big mistake. The buck broke out on the other side of the valley. We had no one covering that area. The buck flushed, traveling south along a gravel road with Jim in hot pursuit.

Mike and Chuck didn't say anything, but their looks gave away their thoughts. They were wondering what they should do. Finally, I said, "Let's gut this buck of Chuck's. Let Jim see if he can run as fast as a deer."

We gutted the buck and were about to load him when a couple of game wardens pulled up. They registered the buck, looking around a little. We figured one of the cars that drove by while we were gutting the buck had called them. Figured we were shooting a doe or must be guilty of something.

Once they were satisfied we weren't criminals, they congratulated Chuck on his first buck. Then, it was time to find our runaway hunter. We loaded up the buck, heading north down the road. There was a sharp corner about a half mile down. When we reached it, we spotted blood on the road.

We got out, and Jim was coming back toward the road. Floyd asked, "Where is he?"

"A guy shot him just before the tower hill."

"Well, I could have told you that the hyenas are always patrolling that old tower road. "Jim, I tried to stop you."

"I saw you. I know I screwed up."

"He had more horns than the fork, but I believe the fork buck was as big as he was."

"Did you get the fork buck?"

"Chuck got him."

We walked over to the truck, and Chuck showed Jim the buck. "He is a nice buck," Jim replied.

Chuck smiled. "He'll be good eating."

"I think one of those goddamn Pierces shot my buck," Jim said.

I knew he was upset, and I said, to lighten him up a little, "What's the most disgusting thing on a woman?"

"It's a Pierce," Jim said.

We all laughed. I put my hand on Jim's shoulder as

I told him what John Peoples had said years ago. "You know there are two types of women in this world. There are the good old big ones and the big old good ones."

"Well, I never thought about it that way, but you're right."

John Peoples was a friend I met in advanced infantry training while in Fort Lewis, Washington. John was a heck of a nice guy. He gambled a little when we had some downtime. However, he never spent any of his winnings, saving them for leave when we finished our training.

Before shipping us to Vietnam, we had gone up to Seattle International Airport to go home for a bit of leave. We'd sat our heavy duffel bags down to check in for our flight. When we returned, his bag was missing. Most of his money and his orders for deployment were in the bag.

The steam was venting out his ears, and he was more than mad. If he'd caught the folks that stole his bag, they would have gotten the beating of their lives.

Security told us that hippies hung around the airport and stole bags from soldiers. They liked to wear combat uniforms to protest the war. My flight was ready to go, so I had to say goodbye to John.

"Did you ever see him again?" Jim asked.

"No, I never saw John again. I don't know if he even made it back from the war. But I think you might be wrong about that guy being a Pierce. They hunt like lions, not hyenas. Dad used to run with the Pierce family in his younger days. I remember him talking about

Red, Whitie, and Blackie Pierce. They're good old local boys that wouldn't steal another lion's buck."

Jim was wrong in more ways than one. Flushing the buck wasn't his biggest mistake. Shooting into a drive that your two brothers are making is just plain stupid. He got excited and didn't consider his shooting lane before firing.

Then old Chuck lost his cool and ran right up on the buck I shot. If that buck had any lead left in his pencil, he'd have gotten up and taken off.

That is why I've always hated driving deer with many guys. Jump hunting with a partner makes for a much safer hunt. You don't need all those hunters if you use your brain a little. Thank God we never had any accidents with our gang.

My prosthetist—for those who don't know what a prosthetist is, it's a person who makes artificial legs and arms—also has one leg off and was hunting over by Necedah Refuge one time. Some boys were making a drive. A deer came out between him and the standers. They opened fire, shooting him in the one good foot he had left. We laughed about it, but it sure in the hell wasn't funny. A little heavier round might have taken the leg off. I know the .45 carbines I hunted with would have done severe damage. He did heal up. Thank God the doctors saved his foot.

Jim was settling down. We all were ready for something to eat, so we went back to the trailer to grab a bite. Mike and Chuck packed up, leaving for home shortly after. I noticed the buck's head hanging out the tailgate when they rounded the corner for their trip home. I was so glad Chuck got the opportunity to hunt with our family. Unfortunately, he never hunted again and died of prostate cancer a few years later. He wasn't a deer hunter but hunted with the lions for that season.

Mike continued to hunt with us for years without a lot of success. His son, Tony, and son-in-law, Scott, join him in later years. The reason for their poor success was that landowners in Monroe County had posted all the private land. The only place left for them to hunt was in public hunting areas. Eventually, they found a place to hunt in Buffalo County. Mike shot a beautiful fifteen-point buck in Buffalo County with his bow. Tony, his son, became hooked on the sport and has taken some good bucks. They've become a hunting family enjoying their time together in the wild country of Wisconsin.

On Thanksgiving, I hunted the area where I'd taken the green fork buck we threw away. It was a lovely day with no snow that year. I sat most of the morning on a stand. Then, I just walked back to the car. I sat on the bank of an old gravel road, waiting for my brother-in-law. It was nearly noon, almost time for turkey and watching football.

A volley of shots rang out across the road from where I sat. I got ready and saw a buck coming straight down the hill right at me. When he reached the road, he stopped to see if any cars were coming. I had my gun on him and pulled the trigger. Down he went, sliding down the bank onto the side of the road.

He never moved; the buck was dead on arrival. He

was a nice eight-point. The buck was delivered right to the road, just in time for Thanksgiving dinner. A hunter appeared from where the shots had come from earlier. He was the guy who'd shot at him. "Nice buck you got there. Do you mind if I take a look at him?" he asked.

"No, do you think you hit him?"

"Well, just wondering if I'd punched a hole in him."

I turned him over so he could get a good look at him. I saw no holes except the one I'd drilled in the front shoulder. So if he hit him, it must have been in the bunghole.

"Darn it, and he was standing when I took my first shot. I missed him completely."

"Well, I've done that more than once myself. Unfortunately, there is more room around a buck than there is in them."

"Congratulations, you've got a good one there. Need any help loading him?"

"Thanks, my brother-in-law is hunting on the other side of the road. He should be along soon. Good luck. I hope you get one."

I had just finished gutting him out when my brother-in-law showed up. We loaded him and headed for home. The turkey must be about ready. Well, that was easy!

After the season, I ran into Bud Forschler. He agreed that it wasn't the Pierce bunch that tagged the buck Jim shot. Instead, he told me he'd found several bucks dead in the valleys along the old tower road over the years.

After the leaves fell off, the hyenas would drive along the road, watching the valleys. They'd shoot a deer and didn't even know enough to look for them. They figured they'd missed if the buck didn't fall dead on sight.

Bud and Dad were good friends most of their lives. I remember Bud coming to the house in the summer with a new riding pony. He was telling Dad how fast the pony was. Dad took the bait, offering to race him with King, our pony.

He saddled up King, and they started down the road like a couple of kids. King was the kid's pony who didn't like being ridden by adults. He was as gentle as a lamb around kids, but the weight of an adult made him uneasy.

Starting the race in the driveway, they'd made their way to the first right turn in the road. They were neck and neck as they approached a bend in the gravel road. The road turned right, and King turned left, throwing Dad onto the gravel roadway. Dad let out a volley of swear words. Bud stopped, laughing his ass off. Dad limped back to the house, screaming at us to get the blanking horse.

We never told Dad that we'd ride the old King up to the farm next to us every day. No one lived there, and ripe grapes were waiting. The driveway to the farm was a left turn at the corner. So the old King figured he knew where Dad was going, and he was helping out.

He was the most intelligent horse we ever owned. I remember riding him in the woods. I'd ridden under a low-hanging branch that knocked me off. He stopped right away and looked back at me to say, "What are you doing down there?"

Dad told us he got him from a guy who gave rides to kids at county fairs. Norbert was just a baby, not more than two years old. My dad would put Norbert on King and let go of the reins. That horse would gently walk around the front yard. Never once did he knock him off. King was 100 percent a kid's pony.

He was over twenty years old when he got down in the barn and couldn't get back up. So Dad had to shoot the dear boy to end his suffering. My mother told me that all Irish people go to heaven and that King was an Irishman's horse, so I shouldn't worry. He'd be in heaven when I arrived. I suppose Dad and Mom are taking good care of him for me.

6

WHO DO THE DEER BELONG TO?

This story is for the king's children.

A vixen fox named Nibbles had four small pups to feed. On her nightly forage, she crossed several farms looking for supper. Crossing the first farm, she met Maxwell, a coyote. She asked, "Can I hunt rabbits on this farm?"

Maxwell replied, "No, this is my hunting grounds, you'll have to move on."

So Nibbles moved to the next farm, where she ran into a badger named Grumpy. She asked Grumpy, "Can I hunt rabbits on this farm?"

"Well, of course not. This farm is my hunting ground. Move on immediately."

Nibbles hung her head and moved on to the next farm. Spotting a rabbit, she gave chase and caught it in just a few short bounds. She turned to go home and ran directly into a wolf named Tucker. He roared, "What do you think you're doing hunting on my farm?"

"Tucker, I have four pups to feed and need this rabbit for supper."

Tucker said, "Drop the rabbit now, or I'll rip you to pieces."

"Tucker," she pleaded, "my pups need food."

"I don't care, this hunting land belongs to me. So drop it and get off my hunting grounds."

Fearing for her life, she dropped the rabbit and moved on to another farm. She noticed this farm didn't have any other predators. At last, she could hunt for supper. Her nose picked up the smell of fresh meat. She followed it to a small metal trap with a piece of meat in the center. *Snap!* Whoops, she had forgotten about the kings of Monroe County.

Nibbles could not escape the clever trap the king had set. She cried, "Please, can someone help me?" After an hour of trying to free herself, Nibbles passed out from exhaustion.

When she awoke, she was with her pups on a new farm. While she was sleeping, a little boy named Kurt Brownell found her. After searching for several hours, he also found her pups. Kurt moved the family of foxes to land the Mississippi Valley Conservancy had set aside.

Kurt spent the rest of his life working to improve conditions for all of God's creatures. Children, do you want to be like Maxwell, Grumpy, Tucker, or the king? Wouldn't the planet be better off if you were more like Kurt? The end!

The days of walkabouts were coming to an end. Indeed, driving deer was out of the question. Rich folks were buying up more and more of the wooded land. The state raised the fines for trespassing to satisfy greedy landowners. The attitude was that the land belonged to them, and everything on it was theirs.

Feeding stations and houses in the woods were starting to appear. This destroyed hunting as I knew it growing up in Wisconsin. You had to get permission from landowners before hunting. Well, that didn't work. They all said no. They hadn't bought the land to share hunting rights with others.

With all the private land closed to hunting, we decided to hunt conservation land south of town. The DNR began an early season hunt for doe. Being disabled, I had the privilege to also tag a buck during this hunt.

Floyd knew how to get into a stand that wasn't too far from the road. The hills were brutally steep on that land.

I believe the federal government was going to put a dam in that area at one time. They bought up a lot of land, later deciding not to go ahead with the project. They must have given it to the state. It was a beautiful piece of land but difficult for a disabled person to hunt.

When we arrived, it was snowing lightly, with just a trace of snow on the ground. I maneuvered my way down alongside a cornfield to the wood line. I'd set up in the woods, not more than one hundred yards from the cornfield. Any further would have been fruitless. The land had more hunters on it than the hair on a blue-tick hound back.

I thought I'd just stay on the fringes. The boys

would all sit down in the valleys. It was quiet until around eight o'clock, when I heard some shooting to the south of me. Nothing came through, so I figured they'd shot a doe or fawn.

The leaves had fallen off the hardwood trees, leaving an incredible valley view. I could see for at least three hundred yards. I was out on a point, with the hill receding to the north of my position.

I heard a deer coming from the north. He came from the only place he could have without me seeing him. It was a good-size buck running slowly in the black brush cover. He circled below me and started back.

I was following him with the scope when he stopped. The crosshairs were on his front shoulders, so I pulled the trigger. Instead of going down, he began to run. I pulled the trigger again. This shot stopped him, and down he went like a sack of potatoes.

I could see he was done for it, so I did my best to stay on my feet sliding down the hill. When I got to him, another hunter came around the hillside. "What did you get there?"

"It's a nice buck."

He closed in on me, breathing hard, and spit out what he couldn't wait to tell me. "This is a doe-only season. You can't take a buck."

"Relax." I pulled up my pant leg and showed him my artificial leg. "This says I can."

"Oh, I didn't realize disabled hunters could shoot a buck in this season."

"Well, most of them can't." I laughed.

"Do you need any help with getting him out of here?"

He helped me gut the buck. When his hunting partner came along, he was ready to pull it to the top of the hill. "What's up? A buck in doe-only season?" he asked, a confused look on his face.

The guy helping me said to him, "This guy got one swinging." I was unsure what I had that was swinging. He must have meant my artificial leg. These boys had a language only they understood.

He said to his partner, "Help me pull him to the top of the hill." Then, he turned to me and asked, "Do you need help getting to the top of the hill?"

"No, I'm good."

I always kidded about bringing two ropes into the woods. One was for the deer, the other rope I'd hook around my neck. On this day, that wouldn't have been a bad idea. If you look at the front inside cover of this book, the top left rack was that buck.

The guys were more than helpful in getting that buck out to the field for pickup. I thanked them, promising the drinks were on me if I ever ran across them in a bar. They thanked me for my service to the country, called me sir, and left.

The real story about disabled hunters is that very few score a decent buck in any season. Some kings support the effort, but most do not include anyone in their hunts but their family.

Floyd came along in about a half hour, and we loaded the buck. He hadn't seen a live hair in the woods. However, he commented that there were many hunters down in the valley. Someone had shot a nice spike buck and left it lying just around the hill from me.

I was about to say I didn't hear anyone shoot, when I remembered the earlier shots. "I did hear them shoot early. So it was a spike buck they shot."

"Right, it was a good one."

"Too bad he'll just go to waste now."

Floyd hunted on private land closer to Wilton the next day. His brother-in-law had a couple of farms with dairy operations. He had taken a good-size doe, so we both had meat.

I like canned venison, and I put up several quarts, cut some lovely strips of meat off the hindquarters, and ground the rest. Floyd was big on chili meat; he ate a lot of venison chili in his life. I'd put my canned venison in a slow cooker with onions, potatoes, and carrots and let it stew for a couple of hours before adding my seasonings.

We'd hunted small game in the woods earlier that season where I shot my buck. I shot a partridge, and Floyd hit a couple of squirrels. We went to the truck, loaded up, and started to leave. A truck pulled in behind us. I thought nothing of it until they kept following us. I slowed down, but they wouldn't pass.

They followed us for a couple of miles. Finally, I stopped and rolled down the window. They stopped, and I motioned for them to drive forward. They slowly drove by the truck, with skulls on their faces. They gave me the finger.

OK, I thought, *now that we have that out of the way, what's your problem?* They just kept on going. I turned to Floyd. "Do you know those guys?"

"No, I never saw them before. There are probably drunks from Wilton."

"How can you tell?"

He laughed, with no answer.

"Well, if you ask me, they look like they might have been in the movie *Deliverance*. What a couple of ass-holes."

"We might have crossed private land going into the public land."

"Those boys didn't look smart enough to own land. I'll bet they have all their money invested in Budweiser beer cans. They're probably saving them up for retire-ment. They must be part of the self-appointed Monroe County pseudobiologists who wander the county."

The ridiculous behavior of people has ruined the sport. It's become a contact sport, like these two guys trying to intimidate us over small game hunting. Neigh-bors and even families fight over hunting rights. A misguided bunch of hunters is in the woods these days. It's good to have lived when people treated animals and each other with some degree of respect.

Remember when Chai Vang shot six hunters to death and seriously wounded two others? What a tragedy for the families. For what? A tree stand. The alarming fact is that I believe it still could happen today, given the right circumstances.

An unhealthy attitude by self-appointed kings has fueled a movement to control deer. Boys are wearing coonskin caps with flags sewn onto their shirts. They believe they're intelligent. Just kidding, I don't want a visit from the Proud Boys.

There has been an ill wind blowing in our nation for some years. Hunters do not realize that they do not own wild things. It's every person's responsibility to look after the wild.

Predators support an intact ecosystem. You might think you know how to manage deer better than natural predators. Unfortunately, you'd be wrong. Predators have evolved over thousands of years to balance nature.

First, the top predators are denied a place at the table. Next, anyone who doesn't own land is banned from the opportunity to hunt. Lastly, the whole resource is destroyed. If you act like a king, you're just hastening the death of the sport.

My Venison Stew

- 1 large onion
- 4 potatoes
- 4 carrots
- 2 lbs. 1-inch venison cubes
- 1 can cream of mushroom soup
- 1 can chicken or beef stock
- Sea salt to taste
- Pepper to taste
- 1 teaspoon garlic powder

I use canned venison. Then, I hold back half the chicken stock until the end. This lets me control the thickness of the stew.

If you prefer noodles, it's the same recipe without potatoes. Be careful not to overdo the noodles. You know they suck up a lot of the juices. You might need to add a little water, of course, and put them in at the end of the cooking time. My wife will also add a cup of sour cream to the pot.

There must be a hundred different takes on this receipt. The one constant is the mushroom soup. How did people exist before Campbell's soup company sold it? I'm careful about adding too much seasoning to the dish. I want the favor of the meat to come through.

If you're using fresh meat, start it first, then add veggies a little later. Cut all the meat and veggies about the same size. Don't get too fussy; this is a man cooking, after all. It goes well with beer for those guys saving Budweiser beer cans for retirement. You could even pour the beer right into the pot.

Floyd's Chili

- 1 large onion
- 4 ribs of celery
- 1 large red bell pepper
- 2 lbs. ground venison
- 1 large can diced tomatoes
- ½ can of water
- 1 small can tomato sauce
- ½ pack chili mix
- 1 can chili beans
- 1 T oil
- Salt
- Pepper
- Chili power
- 1 T sugar

Start with frying cut-up veggies and meat until tender. Use a little oil to start; venison is dry meat with little fat. Add the tomatoes, tomato sauce, and water. I rinse the cans back and forth to get all the good stuff. Add your dry mix, and hold the sugar and beans for now. Get everything boiling, then turn it down to a simmer. Set the timer for one hour and have a beer.

When you come back half drunk, add the beans. You know beans won't take very long. You're just warming them. Wait another ten minutes to taste. Tomatoes can be a little bitter; the sugar sweetens the pot. Add sugar to taste, and simmer for another fifteen minutes.

Put any topping on the chili you like, such as raw onions, hot peppers, cheese, or sour cream. Then, drink the rest of your twelve-pack of Budweiser. The chili gets better with each can you drink.

7

FORT MCCOY'S DISABLED HUNT

The following year, I'd hunt on Fort McCoy for the disabled hunt. It was held early in the season to take advantage of the weather conditions. We had to attend a briefing before the hunt. Kim Mello did the briefing to square away the hunting protocol for the guys. I sensed right from the get-go that this would be a good hunt. Kim was a dedicated biologist and very skillful in customer relations. Volunteers were available to help if a disabled hunter didn't have a partner for the hunt.

The opener was cloudy with a bit of rain. I saw a few does and fawns riding around the roads. We sat out for a good share of the day, but nothing moved. Of course, the rain and the warm temps didn't help. But then, there was very little hunting pressure in the woods.

The second day started with the same weather pattern. We'd hunted on the northeast side of the fort in the morning, seeing nothing. So after lunch, we decided to hunt on the northwest end of the impact area. The area was hilly with oak trees full of acorns. Our thought was maybe those acorns would draw in deer.

We knew a spot where the deer crossed. I have seen as many as forty-five deer cross in one morning in that spot. However, after the wolves took up residence at Fort McCoy, the number of deer crossing there plummeted quickly.

The plan was that Floyd would travel a little north of my position. He'd do some scouting for a bow stand. He'd bring the Ridgeline back to me before dark when he finished. I struggled with two walking sticks to get to the top of a hillside that ran along the road. Once there, after twenty minutes, the squirrels started to feed.

I move a couple of times to find just the right hiding place. Finally, I pulled out my bag of treats and picked a hard candy to suck on. I must have sat there for an hour and a half. A red-tailed hawk flew over, and the squirrels disappeared. A little later, a flock of turkeys came up the valley. They entertained me for fifteen minutes before disappearing over the hill.

Another hill that adjoined the hill I was sitting on ran north. I saw a flash of a deer coming down that side hill. It was a doe; she went to the road and stopped before crossing. I could have taken her, but something told me not to shoot.

In a few minutes, another doe did the same. I also let her cross without shooting. Then, a truck pulled up on the blacktop road and shut off its engine. He must have seen the deer cross. I figured it was one of the disabled hunters that couldn't get out of the truck.

Looking back toward the hill where I'd seen the doe come in from, I saw movement. A darn nice buck came in, stopping just over a mound of dirt. I could not see him but knew exactly where he was. In any direction he ran, I'd have a shot.

The truck started its engine, turning into the valley. I walked up. An old fire lane ran up to the bottom of the hill. My heart sank. I thought for sure the buck would go back. I got my gun ready for a shot in case he decided to retreat. The truck slowly drove up the valley, turned around, and drove back to the road.

They stopped; I thought they might have seen the buck. But no shooting, and I didn't see the buck run. But, dang it, the buck must be standing not more than fifty yards from them. When they hit the blacktop road, they turned to go west.

I heard some leaves rustle where the buck was hiding. The buck came barreling up over that hill right at me. He'd stood there watching the truck for ten minutes before he moved, smart enough to know they hadn't seen him.

I was shaky from the suspense of the last ten minutes. The buck was coming right at me very fast. There was no time to waste. Keeping cool enough to get the job done, I pulled down on his front—the gun went *boom*, and the deer fell not more than fifty feet from me. I'd hit him right at the base of the neck.

He was dead within ten seconds, never even turned over. Take a look at the front inside cover of this book. He's on the top right-hand side. He was a beautiful eight-point, a buck to remember. The meat off him was delicious, unlike some old bucks in the late-season rut.

He was a brute; I could hardly move him. So finally, after gutting him, I shouted for Floyd to come. I figured he'd put him out for me. Well, no response, so after fifteen minutes of screaming, I gave up. I thought maybe I could pull this boy downhill.

I took my gun to the tree line that bordered the road, returning to start my pull. The rain was falling lightly, making the leaves slick. I grabbed onto the buck's horns and pulled. I couldn't move him. I had a rope, so I attached it to his horns. I still couldn't get enough leverage with my artificial leg to move him.

I sat down, out of breath, and screamed as loud as I could for Floyd. No answer. Well, he'll be back before dark, I thought. I walked to a tree, bracing myself on the backside of it. I pulled as hard as possible, and he came right to me. Now, is there another tree I could reach from here?

Sure enough, I found one, so I reached that tree with my buck. Unfortunately, the next tree wasn't in line with the road, so I had to zigzag back and forth to the road. It was going pretty well until I ran out of the hill. The last hundred yards to the road, the ground was flat.

It was much harder to pull him on flat ground. I was exhausted. The rain picked up, and I decided that was far enough. Floyd came along about a half hour before shooting time was over.

I sat on a hump just out of the woods. "What did you get?"

"Well, come look for yourself."

When he got to the buck, he could not believe his eyes. "Holy shit, you got a nice one."

"Not bad for a guy with one swinging."

I was so tired I could hardly get to the truck. Floyd pulled the buck halfway to the truck, and two trucks stopped on the road. One was the truck I'd seen earlier in the fire lane. The guys got out to help Floyd load the buck.

"You know this buck was standing not more than fifty yards from you guys when you turned around on the fire lane earlier."

"You're kidding."

"No, I'm not. This boy bolted right over me when you turned the truck onto the blacktop."

"I heard you shoot. Well, congratulations, nice damn buck."

That's one thing I always appreciated about Fort McCoy's disabled hunts. The guys were happy to help the disabled hunter. They were supportive of each other. If you got a buck, it was a celebration for all. They hunted as a team, one healthy hunter paired with a disabled hunter.

Another great thing about the disabled hunt was that not many hunters were on McCoy. Maybe thirty or so were all that would show. That left thousands of acres to hunt without crowding someone else. I've also hunted on McCoy in the nine-day hunt. It's so crowded the first day you can't find a place to stand. After the first day, it's pretty quiet until Thanksgiving.

McCoy is constantly changing to accommodate the

perceived current needs of the military. I believe many areas have been overdeveloped. Too many special range sites, in my opinion. They need to leave the spaces as wild as possible. The natural resource folks do their best to keep the wild places pristine. Still, they're fighting an uphill battle with a culture of ignorance—enough editorializing.

I hunted McCoy for many of the disabled hunts over the years, taking several does and some good bucks. I can't remember in detail most of them. However, one I'll tell you about stood out because of the circumstances of the hunt.

On opening morning, we'd gone north almost to the end of McCoy. There was an area that had many deer trails running across the road. It was low land with thick swamps. You could hardly see the deer. We arrived early, and I took a stand not very far off the road.

We had sat there for a half hour when another truck pulled up. The truck parked not more than fifty yards from our vehicle. Two guys got out, taking a stand very close to us. I thought, *You've got thousands of acres to hunt and have to sit on my lap.* I figured the boys didn't understand how deer hunting works. Maybe it was city boys on their first hunt.

We sat there for about fifteen minutes. Finally, we were ready to get up to give them some space. We'd take the truck and find another spot. I saw something move from behind their sitting position. It was a doe with a spike buck following.

The disabled hunter sat there watching the deer go

by, never raising his gun. *Interesting, I wonder what he is waiting for.* The doe out front snorted as they came running at me. I didn't have a safe shooting lane with them directly in line with the shot. I waited for the deer to go by to take my shot.

Boom! Just the one shot was all I got at the buck. It looked like a good shot, but he didn't show any signs of being hit. Still, I was pretty sure I'd hit him. So the guys came over, and the disabled hunter said, "They were doe, and you missed it."

"Well, you could be right, but that one was a small buck."

"Nah, I saw no horns on him."

"You guys plan on hunting here this morning? Because we'd be glad to give you a little room after we take a look to see if we have any blood on the ground."

"No, that's all right. We're going to get some breakfast."

"Well, good luck. I hope you get one."

They loaded up, and off they went. Floyd looked at me and commented, "They're going for breakfast at this time on the opener?"

"I think those boys are a little new to hunting deer? It's been long enough. Let's go see if we have a deer."

We checked out the spot I'd visually marked in my head where I took the shot. We made a couple of circles and still couldn't find blood. I was pretty sure I'd punched a hole in him. "What do you think, Floyd? Want to take this thick grass swamp to the road? I can circle out and set up on the road."

"Sure, I'll wait a few minutes for you to get set up, and I'll bring it down."

I hurried along, careful not to get too close to the swampy grassland. I took a stand where the shooting would be perpendicular to the road. I didn't want to shoot straight down the road with all the disabled hunters driving around. I also needed to be aware of Floyd's location.

I sat there for about five minutes when I heard Floyd shout, "You got him!" I followed the sound of his voice for about one hundred fifty yards. The buck was on a deer trail without a speck of blood on the ground. Sure enough, it was a good shot in the front quarter. The shot might have been just a hair too far back, but respectable considering the buck was on the run.

"I can't believe you couldn't find any blood on the ground."

"This is a Fort McCoy buck. He might be full of sand," Floyd said.

"He's a little smaller than I thought he was."

"Well, they all look bigger when running through the woods. That's why the big ones always get away."

We gutted the boy, loaded him up, and headed back to the check-in station. The two hunters that had gone for breakfast were there chatting. They came over. "That wasn't the one we saw go by us, was it?"

"Yes, it was. My brother took the swamp back to the road and found him lying. He never bled a drop, not even when he hit the ground."

I'm positive those two hunters had never shot a deer

in their lives. Sometimes it can be easy to kill a deer, but you can't shoot them in a restaurant. They needed an experienced hunter to teach them how to hunt. Their hunting outfits were a giveaway—expensive clothing with no bloodstains. A country boy would have had a few rips in his clothing, or his hat would have been frayed on the brim.

A cameraman from the public affairs office drove up. He wanted a shot of a disabled hunter with a deer. I was the only one there, so he took my picture. I had to tell him the story; I included Floyd's contribution to the successful hunt.

They ran it in the next issue of the post paper. It was good PR for them and good that disabled hunters saw they could get one. So many of them take a doe or fawn right off the road. I never cared about shooting from the car. I'm not knocking them for it; I just liked a little more challenge than that.

One of the guys hunting in the disabled hunt was in a wheelchair. I had seen him sitting along a fire lane in his chair, waiting for one to cross. He was on a pretty darn good stand. He hunted with his father-in-law. They were a great team. I liked their style of hunting. I don't know if he ever got one or not, but they hunted like lions, not hyenas.

I'm sure I would have never killed the eight-point buck from the car. That buck watched until the truck left the area. He knew what cars meant and wasn't volunteering to come to supper. Fawns will stand around the roads, especially after losing their mothers. I've shot a few fawns in my life, but not many, and I wouldn't think of shooting one now.

I bet a lot of them don't make it to adulthood. Without the old doe, they're easy prey for any predator. I guess we all need our mothers until we've grown. I don't know about you, but I'm still sucking my thumb. I did get over trilling my hair last year.

On one of the disabled hunts, I hadn't gotten off the road very far when I took a stand. Three fawns crossed the road and started to feed. They were just behind a thin ribbon of black brush running along the road. I'd seen these little guys on the open day with their mother. Then, just after passing me, a guy shot their mother.

I was watching them when an SUV pulled up. It stopped, and the window came down. A barrel appeared, then a loud *boom*—one of the fawns went down, another *boom* the other fawn went down. The third one ran by me. The guy had shot the second fawn in the hindquarter, and it was still alive.

The door opened, and out came a guy that must have gone three hundred and fifty pounds. He came tearing through the black brush like a bull elephant.

He finally saw me and shouted, "Did I get it?"

"Yep, you sure did." He was on them like white on rice. He reshot the wounded one in the front shoulder, leaving a nasty hole in it. Well, at least the poor thing was dead. With the holes he had in those fawns, he could have eaten both in one sitting. I didn't get a close look at his rifle, but it was big. It might have been a 7mm Mag.

He never said another word to me. He just pulled the two fawns to the SUV to gut. I thought this guy didn't look very disabled, but then the door on the other side of the truck opened and a disabled hunter got out and limped around the truck.

Did this guy think he was fooling someone? The fat boy was the one that shot the deer. There was no way the disabled hunter sitting in the other seat did. He hadn't seen me sitting just beyond the fawns in an orange outfit. I didn't turn him in, but after thinking about it, I wished I had. I believe the fat boy should have been ticketed for shooting the fawns. Fort McCoy had gone to all the effort to put on a disabled hunt, and this joker pulled this crap. I guess all sports have a few idiots that abuse the rules. Ninety-nine percent of the guys on this hunt were outstanding sportspeople. The real trouble with guys like that is he was giving the disabled hunting a black eye.

I'm a believer in letting hunters do their own thing. I try very hard not to apply my standard to others. I believe hunters should adhere to fair chase principles. If they are disabled, the principles of the fair chase can be flexible depending on their condition. I'd encourage disabled hunters to make the hunt as challenging as possible.

If you get a deer, that's great. If you don't get a deer, that's also great. You got out in the wild with a trusted friend and hunted like a lion. You gave it your best shot. Bucks are the gold medals of disabled hunting. If you take a nice doe, that's a silver medal. The important thing is to do it yourself in a sporting manner.

8

THINGS THAT WENT WRONG WHILE BOW HUNTING

Bow hunting did a lot of good for the sport of deer hunting, and it did a lot of bad. In some ways, hunters became better hunters. They paid more attention to scent, movement, and camouflage. As leagues formed, hunters became proficient with their bows.

Now, on the other hand, many ridiculous, destructive activities increased, which altered the fair chase rules of hunting. Hunters became couch potatoes, sitting in tree stands, which morphed into tree houses. Then, trail cameras became popular, and they watched deer twenty-four seven.

Hunters began to feed deer piles of corn and apples. The deer would visit these piles of feed every evening. Deer bunched up in pockets around the feed, waiting for their appointment with death. Either from an arrow or from chronic wasting disease.

These misguided coach potatoes with their high-tech devices are not hunters at all. They are hyenas pretending to be lions. When the deck is that stacked against the prey, it's slaughter, not hunting. You'd have the same amount of fun building a tree stand in the barnyard, and beef would also be much better eating.

Take a look at the ten-point buck on the inside front cover. He is the biggest buck I have ever killed with anything. Although not the biggest I ever saw, that was my first story. The great thing about bagging him was that I shot him with my ten-point crossbow.

We'd been hunting for about a week in the early season. One Friday night, Kim Mello, my wife, Shi, and I decided to go out for fish. We stopped at the local tavern on Superior Avenue. Two of the local boys were talking about hunting deer on McCoy. They were telling of a big buck they'd seen a couple of times.

Moe Amundson was bitching out the other guy for not taking a smaller buck. Kim commented, "Where are you boys hunting?"

"We're hunting just across from the pine plantation. You know, where the Martin boys hunt."

"Right," Kim said.

I never said a word, but I knew where the Martin boys hunted. We'd also hunted in that area before. The trouble with the place is that it lies right along the freeway. It was impossible to hear anything in the woods. The woods were very long and narrow, very unimpressive for a bow hunt.

They continue to drink and rave about the Bullwinkle buck taunting them. So I began to think Floyd and I would give Bullwinkle a go the next night. If the buck was that nice, it would be worth spending a little time on him.

It was a gray October day when we pulled onto the road to hunt. There was a white grass field on the north side of the road. The big buck ran across the road just after we drove past it. His head was down, so it was hard to see horns, but I knew it was the one they had talked about.

"God, that's a nice buck."

"A nice buck, OK. What's the plan?" Floyd asked.

"I think we should drive on a little and watch for his trail. You know they set up a rut trail and check it out daily."

We drove down the road slowly until spotting a trail going across the road. Floyd decided to take it down to find a stand. I turned the truck around and drove back up the road. I figured the buck would circle the white grass field. I've seen them do it many times, and they'll make a rutted trail just inside the tree line around a field.

After I cleared the field, I found a trail crossing the road. I drove down a bit before stopping. I didn't want to stink up the trail, so I planned to circle wide of it. I loaded up my bow and rubbed a little grease on the rails. Checked my arrow over darn good before loading it. Things were good; the equipment was ready to go. I spray a little scent killer on my clothing.

The ground was perfect for a disabled hunter, flat with a bit of brush. After getting into the woods, I began to scan for downed trees. They were my favorite place to hide. I couldn't climb a tree, so natural ground blinds worked well.

I picked up a few scrapes and a couple of small deer trails. I could tell he'd been in here. The tracks were large. The scrapes also looked like a good buck had made them. I must have spent another fifteen minutes looking for just the correct setup.

I found fresh deer droppings on the trail. This hunt just kept getting better. I'd passed up a couple of downed trees and was ready to go back when I spotted a massive oak that had tipped over.

Two deer trails crossed about thirty yards from the downed oak. From my backside, nothing could see me sitting. I checked the wind. Good, it was coming out of the south. I found a small limb and sat down, thinking I was ready to rock and roll.

I had trouble turning to shoot once on the ground with the damn artificial leg, so I cleaned away any obstructions close to me. Then, I had enough room to maneuver a little if I had to. I carried a small, light-weight square of camouflage with me. I spotted a few small branches and hooked the camouflage to them.

I might have sat there for twenty minutes before I had to cough. I tried my best to make it sound like a buck grunting. Well, surprise, surprise—I heard a reply. Something grunted back at me.

Holy blank, was that a buck behind me? I got the bow ready, froze in place, and didn't even turn my head. I saw him coming around the tree from the corner of my eye. His horns were the first thing I saw.

There was a small brush between him and me. I was afraid that my arrow might hit one of them. I shouldered the bow and released the safety. He kept walking until he reached the intersection of the two deer trails.

There he turned right at me. Shit, I didn't want a straight-on shot. He stopped, looking right at me. I was busted. Pretty sure he was about too bold, so I took my shot. I aimed exactly dead center between the legs, about heart high.

When the bow went off, he was in the process of bolting. His head came down as he loaded those hind legs to run. It all happened so fast that I didn't get a good view of where the arrow landed. I knew it had found a good landing place, but was it a killing shot?

I sat there for a few minutes in shock. What a nice buck, and I'd coughed him in. I'd done everything right, so I didn't want to blow it now. I sat there for at least fifteen minutes. I figure it wasn't long enough to track yet, but I'd look where he was standing.

There was blood all over. He was bleeding like a stuck pig. I stood there for another ten minutes before I started to track him. It was easy, the blood never let up. Finally, in about three hundred yards, I spotted him.

Those big horns were sticking up off the ground. I stood and watched for a few minutes and said a little thank-you prayer, remembering my best friend, Bill. Finally, I decided the buck was dead. When I got there, I could hardly believe how nice he was.

I looked to see where I'd hit him. The shot was high because he bolted, but the arrow had found an artery.

The arrow tip had stayed long enough to open a good-sized hole in him. He'd bled to death in three hundred yards. It worked out, but it certainly could have gone the other way.

He had run away from the road, and I must have been five hundred yards from the road. I was very close to the freeway. I could hear the semitrucks howling as they downshifted for the grade of a hill.

I gutted him out and tied a rope around his horns. Again, I screamed at Floyd until I was hoarse. He didn't come, so I did my trick of bracing myself against a tree and pulling him.

This worked, but it was slow going. I must have pulled on the buck for two hours and still wasn't to the truck. Finally, I could not go another step. It was starting to get dark. I decided to see if I could drive back into the woods a little.

My truck didn't have four-wheel drive, but the ground was dry. I'd gotten within fifty yards of him with the truck. I could pull him to the truck or hook a rope to the bumper to get him out.

Then Floyd appeared. "What's going on here?"

"I'm just taking a joy ride in the woods."

"You get one?"

"Yes, a nice buck about fifty yards back on that trail."

He laid down his bow and went to retrieve the buck for me. I heard him say, "Damn, nice buck." We both had a time getting him loaded when he got to the truck. Once we had him loaded, we sat on the bumper and talked.

"He's the same ten-point buck that crossed the road when we came in."

"Yes, he just circled that white grass field and came right in on me. I shot him a little high; he bled like a pig."

"Why did you shoot him high?"

"Well, he had me and bolted just as the arrow released."

It was dark by then. We drove over to Kim Mello's house. He aged him for me and said he was between four and five years old. I reminded him of the story we heard in the Uptown bar last Friday night from Moe Amundson. "That's the buck he was talking about."

"Yep, I'm pretty sure this boy was the one they were trying to get."

"What do you think his weight will be?

"I think he'll go pretty close to two hundred pounds." I never did get an official weight on him, but I did can a lot of meat. Floyd and Kim came out and helped butcher him. I gave them both plenty of steaks for their help.

After that, we hunted that woods several times and never saw another deer in it. However, we did hunt across the road from it and saw deer. One of the Martens boys shot a buck and told me where he shot it. "Do you mind if I try hunting in those woods?"

"Of course not." He even told me he'd made a little natural hiding place to hunt from.

The weather was terrible all week, rainy, windy, and warm. Not good conditions for hunting, so we waited all week for the weather to improve. So, finally, we decided to give it a go on Friday.

It was pretty decent when we arrived. First, we set up a couple of natural blinds. Then, after a couple of hours, the wind picked up. *Oh, goody,* I thought, *that will mess up tonight's hunt.*

I sat there until almost dark. Thinking is wasting my time. Then, finally, I got up and walked north toward a fire lane. I was about forty yards away when a buck stepped out of it. He was a six-point within shooting range.

I went down on one knee and braced myself for the shot. But, as I said, it was almost dark. I still had a good bead on him with my scope, so I pulled the trigger, and the arrow went over the buck's body by at least three feet. Then, of course, the buck bolted.

What in the world was wrong with this bow? I took a good look at it. A small stick was in between the string and the rail. When I set up the shot, I must not have noticed the brush sticking up. When the string came forward, it clipped the top of the stick off, affecting the arrow's path.

First, the ten-point buck bolted as I released the shot. Now, it was an unseen brush causing the equipment to malfunction. These mistakes were almost impossible to control. I'm not done. There are more screwups to come.

Floyd and I were hunting north of the impact area on Fort McCoy the following year. It was a bluebird day, and the sun was glimmering off the fall leaves. It had gotten cold the night before and froze. The color was at its peak in the woods.

There wasn't any wind to be concerned over. I believe it was around three o'clock when we arrived. We were already into October, so we were starting to lose daylight hours. We'd seen bucks in this area, just not close enough to shoot. You know how it is with hunting deer with a bow. If it can go wrong, it will.

I sat up on the edge of a thick swamp. A doe with two fawns went by around four o'clock. A family of gray squirrels kept me alert with their constant noise. Time dragged as it sometimes does while hunting. It was a little after five-thirty when an owl hooted to mark the changing light.

The sun had fallen below the tree line, and darkness was coming soon. I decided to make it to the truck while I could still see the trail that ran through the black brush. When I got to a white grass field, I could see three deer feeding. I sat down, resting against a pine tree.

I figured they were the three that crossed earlier on my stand. After a few minutes, I reaffirmed they were.

There was a hole in the forest that the sun shone through from the west. It was dark to the east but still light to the west. I was preoccupied with watching the field, so I didn't look right away when I heard something coming from the west. I figured it was another squirrel finding a nest for a sleepover. When I finally turned, there stood a real beautiful buck. Not sure how many points.

I shouldered my bow; he just stood there. He was also looking at the deer in the field. I put the bead on his front shoulder; balls, I'll get this boy. Slid the safety off, one more careful aim, and let it go.

The arrow left the bow with the sound of a muffled thud. What in the hell? Not again. The buck turned around and ran back into the black brush. I could see he had at least eight points when he came into the light. My heart sank into my stomach.

The commotion spooked the other three deer. They bounded across the field and disappeared. I knew what had happened without even looking. Once again, when I sat down, it was almost dark. I hadn't seen a little brush sticking up between the bowstring and the bow's body.

It was just a tiny stick, not more than one-quarter inch thick. I pulled it out of the ground, figuring I would show Floyd. The story amused him, so at least we laughed. I'm sure anyone who has ever hunted for deer with a bow has such stories to tell.

I came to bow hunting for deer late in my life. As a child, a friend and I used to hunt pheasant with a thirty-pound recurve bow. I lived in Racine at the time, which was a large city. Still, you could hunt in certain areas with a bow at that time.

We'd buy Flu arrows; they have large fletching on them. They might travel fifty yards at the max. We knew the hunting area well and occasionally bagged a rooster or two. Even shot one on the wing once.

It was a cold, snowy morning, and we hunted along a pond with cattails. I could see pheasant tracks all over the place. Finally, a rooster came up right in front of me.

He had trouble getting out of the cattails, so when he cleared the tops of the cattails, I gave him one.

To my surprise, the arrow hit him dead center. He tumbled to the ground. I jumped on him, picked him up, and wrung his neck. After that, we mostly shot rabbits with our bows. They'd sometimes sit too long, thinking they were hidden.

Small game hunting with a bow was more challenging than big game hunting. Of course, nowadays, I don't even think I'd eat a rabbit. However, I did have a friend whose mother could cook rabbits.

She first boiled them in a big pot to tenderize the meat. Then, she'd finish cleaning them, picking out any shot or hair in the flesh. Then, she made a little sauce with spices and onions. Finally, she'd stick them in the oven until they were finger-licking good. Am I making you hungry? I bet they'd taste good with your Budweiser while watching the Packers.

Kim Mello's Venison and Kraut Casserole

- 1 lb. ground venison
- 1 can cream of mushroom soup
- 1 can cream of celery soup
- 1 onion, chopped
- 1 can sweet sauerkraut
- 2 cups mild cheddar cheese, shredded
- 1 cup water or milk
- 2 handfuls of noodles
- Salt and pepper to taste
- Garlic powder, a couple of sprinkles

Brown onions and venison and add salt, pepper, and garlic powder. In a good-size bowl, mix soups, water, and ground venison—place noodles in the bottom of a casserole dish. Pour the soup mixture over the noodles and add kraut. Top everything with cheese. Bake at 350° for forty minutes.

Note: You'll get the hang of how many noodles to put in. If you overdo it, the dish will be dry. It's better after sitting in the refrigerator for a day. You could use regular kraut if you like. A handful of cut-up mushrooms wouldn't hurt anything either.

9

THE WINDY BUCK

Take another look at the wheel on the front of this book. See the horns on the lower right? That's the buck I'll tell you about now. These are just nice racks, taken ethically by a disabled hunter. I shot them on land that belonged to the citizens of the United States of America.

Once again, we were hunting on Fort McCoy's north post along the impact area. We had to be careful not to get too close to the impact area. If you violated that space, the deer would know you were there. I'd seen guys park trucks and put up ground blinds right on the border. Of course, they never saw a deer; even the fawns weren't that dumb.

We'd parked on a sand road far enough away to not spook the deer. Then we made very little noise setting up for the hunt. But of course we never hunted in that area if the wind was blowing from the north. Hunters didn't understand that to kill a buck, you had to do things right.

For this hunt, we'd scouted a little early in the week. A buck was coming out of the impact area, taking the west side of the road into a swamp. Floyd and I set up not too far apart. With bow hunting, you can only cover one hundred yards anyway.

I was on the buck's second rub after leaving the impact area. It was getting to that time of the evening when bucks started to move. The buck crossed a sand border that separated the woods from the impact area. He came into me, stopping about twenty yards away.

He put his head up and started to rub his face on a low-hanging branch. This was the shot I was waiting for. I pulled up the crossbow to aim. Unfortunately, I was sitting at an angle to him, so I couldn't get the bow around to shoot. I would have to readjust my body to get a shot. When I dropped the bow to readjust, he picked me up, bolting. Dang it!

Floyd had also seen him. He wondered why I didn't take a shot. I might have been able to get a picture, but it has to be right with a bow. Otherwise, you'd just wound the buck and never get him. So I felt good about letting him go.

We saw a herd of doe with fawns come off the impact area just before dark. There was one spike buck with them, but too far to shoot. So we wrapped things up for the evening, and it was time for supper.

The buck came off the impact area early. I bet he'd be more careful tomorrow night. We decided to take a look at his rubs the following day. We discovered he was taking the west side of the road out, then back in on the east side of the road.

That afternoon I sat up on the east side of the road. There was a thick line of brush that ran parallel to the road. I was hidden in the back of a small brush pile. I sat there for a couple of hours. Then, I started thinking maybe I'd misread the signs.

Suddenly, the buck came in on me from the swamp, so I was right. He was on his way back into the impact area. The wind was kind of swirling around the hillside I sat on. The buck stopped a hundred yards out, looked right at me, and then ran by me at top speed.

He must have picked up my scent. I remember being uncomfortable with the conditions. Well, just another opportunity lost by wind conditions. But I still felt good about figuring this boy's pattern out. I knew where he'd set up his rut trail.

We decided to pull off this spot for a few days and hunted on the south post without seeing much. Floyd did see a buck with a doe but didn't get a shot. So the following week, we got back to hunting this buck.

It rained in the morning, and the air smelled fresh. We'd gotten set up for the hunt around three-thirty. The wind was coming out of the south. I decided I'd cross the road to try to get him on his way back to the impact area.

As I sat there, the wind increased, and a storm moved in from the west. Finally, around five o'clock, it started to sprinkle. Not a lot of rain, but enough to get everything wet. It would get dark early tonight with the clouds looming overhead.

I sat there for another half hour, watching the swamp for movement. Then, I turned around to look to the south for some reason. I picked up movement about one hundred yards out. It was a deer coming right at me. It came within thirty yards and stopped, turning broadside to me.

It was hard to pick up the horns on a gray night, but they were there. I shouldered my bow. The scope clarified my view. Sure enough, it was the eight-point buck I'd been hunting.

I took careful aim, figuring out which post on the scope to shoot from. Finally, I let an arrow go, and it plucked when it hit him. *Damn, a good shot,* I thought. He swirled, heading back to where he'd come from.

I observed him, visually marking the trail he'd taken. Then, suddenly, I saw him come up in the air and disappear. *What was that?* I thought. My breath came back to normal.

I waited for as long as I dared. It was getting dark. I had to mark the trail for the following day. I figured Floyd and I would return early the next morning to track him. I hoped it wouldn't rain too hard and wash away the blood.

Before cutting into the woods to the stand, I'd walked down a fire lane. When I got to it, he lay right in the middle. I checked out the rack. I'd made a great shot right in the heart. He didn't go over a hundred yards from where I'd shot him. His last jump must have been straight in the air. I had spent time figuring out his pattern, and it paid off.

I let a war hoop out for Floyd. This time he heard me. In a few minutes, he drove the truck down the fire lane. We gutted the buck carefully to avoid getting sand in the meat. My persistence paid off. It took a few tries, but I finally bagged him. His markings gave away his pattern. I just had to stay with it until he made a mistake.

The wind was in my favor that night; there are times when the wind can be good. He would have picked up my scent if I'd come straight into the stand. Instead, those few extra minutes I took circling wide helped me bag the buck. So many hunters mess up the hunt on their way into a stand.

Too much activity by hunters of any kind will spook a buck. You need to scout on the off days. Let the buck come back to his natural pattern. Also, don't broadcast your position to other hunters, especially on Fort McCoy. There are always hungry hyenas looking for a meal.

Like any father, I wanted to share my excitement of hunting with my son. Shawn Lee, my only son, and I have one grandson, Tate Scott Williams. When Shawn was twelve, I introduced him to hunting. I enrolled him in a safety course. He learned the right way to hunt with a high-powered rifle. In the fall, we tried out the gun he would use for the hunt.

On opening day, we hunted north of Tomah on private land. It was hilly country with mostly oak trees. It turned out to be a warm day, but I don't think any of our guys saw deer.

We'd all met back at the trucks around ten o'clock in the morning. Shawn came back without his gun. I asked, "Where is your gun, Shawn?"

"Oh, it was too heavy, so I left it in the woods."

I went off on him, reading him the riot act, and using language I shouldn't have. He then got the gun and returned it to the truck. Steam was coming out of my ears.

I shouldn't have reacted that way; it was my fault for not staying right with him. This time should have been reserved for him alone. The truth was, he wasn't interested in hunting deer at all.

I should have recognized that and found other ways to have some father-son time in the woods. For example, we could have just picked blueberries in good weather.

Anything would have been better than screaming at my son for something I did wrong. Oh well, dads make mistakes. We are genuinely sorry for being such asses.

I remember telling him to go play in the leaves in the backyard when he was a young child. When I looked out to check on him, he'd climbed up the tree and was reading a book. He was always very interested in history and learning of any kind. So I was the dummy, not him, for not seeing who he was.

I also took him fishing. That sport stuck with him. It's challenging to know what children will take up or reject. I had a 50 percent track record on Shawn. Not bad for Dad's firstborn.

Now, with my grandson, the jury is still out. He just graduated from college, so he doesn't hunt or fish at this time. His father and mother divorced early in his life, so Grandpa had the privilege of teaching Tate to fish and hunt. We spent many days together learning these sports.

With grandchildren, you have more time and patience to go with it. So I'd bought him a nice Mathews bow, enrolling him in classes for the summer. He went to practice once a week for months until he was proficient with his bow.

The season had been open for a couple of weeks, so we hunted on McCoy's north post, over on the west side. Floyd was hunting with us that night. He took a stand on a darn nice deer trail.

There was an old apple tree with apples up high on it. The deer had cleaned all the low-hanging fruit off early in the season. I pointed that out to Tate. "Who do you think has been eating all these apples?"

"I think it was a deer, Grandpa."

"So, where are you going to set?"

"I'll set up right behind this downed tree." He sat and knocked an arrow in the bow.

I circled to the north just to stay away from the trail coming from the impact area. I was only about sixty yards from him. I found a perfect log to lie down behind. I gave Tate the old thumbs-up. I motioned for him to watch to the east of his stand.

We hadn't sat there for more than an hour when a ten-point buck came up the trail to the apple tree. He stopped about sixty yards from Tate. Tate saw him and was waiting for him to close. Then, from behind Tate, a herd of deer started to snort. They'd come up another deer trail and had gotten our scent.

Tate looked at me, confused as to what to do. I motioned to him to keep his eyes on the buck. I could have shot the buck, but I was here for Tate this time. I'd learned my lesson from my son, Shawn. The buck stood there for the longest time. That boy wanted to see if there were any apples under that tree.

The herd of deer upwind from Tate kept snorting as they stomped the ground. The buck knew something was wrong. Fortunately, he didn't know what had spooked the doe. We were a bit uphill from him with the wind in our favor. I don't believe he ever knew we were there. The doe finally convinced him to return, and he turned and retreated into the woods.

The memory I have of that time with Tate is more valuable than horns hanging on my back porch. I just wished I'd taken more time with my son to pick blueberries. Your job as a father or grandfather is to make memories with your loved ones. Have you told your son or daughter that you love them today? Well, what are you waiting for?

We stayed until dark before going to get Floyd. When I turned the truck around, the light shone on him, holding on to an eight-point buck. These two boys had come in together. Floyd had seen the ten-point buck come in early with the one he got.

We sat on the tailgate, dangling our feet. Tate told Floyd all the details of the hunt. The stars were bright that night as we loaded the buck for transport. We heard in the distance a howl. It was a perfect ending to a beautiful day of memories. I remarked, "That sounded like a wolf to me."

Floyd replied, "There is no wolf on Fort McCoy."

"Well, if there isn't, the coyotes have learned how to howl like wolves."

The next time Tate and I got out was the opener of the gun season. We decide to hunt along the border of Hall's farm, just on Fort McCoy. Kim Mello, Floyd, his son, Lonnie, Tate, and I hunted together. We'd all driven separately. Floyd, with his son Lonnie, had already gone into the woods when we got there.

Kim sat up one hill over from us. There was snow on the ground. As we walked up the north side of a hill, we sounded like a herd of buffalo crunching our way to the top. We finally got into position, finding a good place to hide among the small pines.

I heard a shot that sounded like it came from where Floyd was standing earlier. Then, another shot came from the private land to the east. I saw movement from the area Kim was standing.

A flash of gray crossed the snow and then disappeared. The snow had melted in spots, leaving oak leaves for a background. I told Tate to get ready. He raised his gun, prepared to aim.

From the valley below came a beautiful gray wolf.

To be sure, I told Tate not to shoot. It was a wolf coming. He came right up to us before putting on the brakes, not more than twenty yards away.

He stopped for a few seconds to plan his escape. It was a male with traditional gray and brown wolf markings. His body rippled with muscles. He was over one hundred pounds. His coat had already filled out for the coming winter.

Tate watched him closely as he circled us, finally disappearing over the ridge.

"What do you think, Tate?"

"Pretty cool, Grandpa. I didn't know there were wolves on Fort McCoy."

"Remember our bow hunt when we saw the ten-point buck?"

"I remember you said that was a wolf howling."

"Tate, not many people in this country have ever seen a wolf in the wild. Consider yourself very lucky; I guess you'll never see another one. It's my first one, and I'm a grandpa."

We saw another rare sighting that morning. About half an hour later, a pileated woodpecker landed on a birch tree branch. It was a beautiful male with all his colors glowing in the sunlight. Of course, there are many more of them, but they can be a little hard to see up close.

I believe they have darn good eyesight. Usually, I hear them or get a glimpse of them at a distance. But, this pretty boy was close, probably sick of flying away from hunters. Anyway, he sat long enough to catch his wind and flew off.

We heard Floyd and Lonnie talking by my truck. We went to see what was up. Floyd had taken a nice four-point buck earlier. They loaded him, then started to trash talk to Tate. He said he'd have to eat the testicles of his first buck. "You want to see what they taste like, Tate?" Floyd asked.

"No thanks, I'm good with waiting for my buck."

"Are you sure?

"Positive."

We all laughed and ate on the back of the pickup truck. Kim's truck was gone. He'd tried a pine plantation just a little down the road. I found out later in the day he'd taken a nice nine-point buck. Good, he got one. This was his first year retired. He always worked on the first day of deer hunting, never getting a chance to hunt.

Tate and I hunted along the Lacrosse River on Fort McCoy on Thanksgiving. The range control folks kept it closed most of the time. I always thought they saved it for their buddies to hunt.

We headed for where I knew the deer had crossed the river. I saw a hunter sitting right along the river in that spot. So, we veered off to the north, taking a stand. In less than an hour, the guy got up and left.

We slowly worked our way down to the south. "Tate, hold up. That guy was too close to the river. We need to stay back a little." I said. We found a comfortable hiding place before sitting down.

About fifteen minutes later, four deer came across the river and over the bank. Tate lowered his gun, shooting one of them. It didn't go down. Instead, it ran toward the impact area. Another three followed. He also hit one of them. It ran around a brush pile and stopped. I pulled down on its neck and finished it off. I didn't want another one running away.

Tate asked, "Grandpa, how did you know the deer would cross the river at that spot?"

"Well, if you look to the west, you'll see a thick brush line going to the impact area. Deer follow the cover, especially during hunting season," I said.

"So, if that other guy would have just waited, he'd gotten a deer?" Tate asked.

"No, he was too close to them; they could smell him and probably heard him leave. They'd been extinct long ago if they were as dumb as that guy hunting them. The deer like to night pasture in the high grass across the creek, then travel to the safety of the impact area in the morning," I said.

Tate asked, "So, deer know the times and areas that are safe?"

"Yes, it has been my observation that hunters underestimate deer intelligence. Deer react to the pressure put on them. I used to see a hundred deer just driving around Fort McCoy. Since bow hunting has started, I'm lucky to see a couple. They now stay up all night drinking with their buddies. When morning comes, they're sleeping in the impact area with a hangover," I said.

"Right, Grandpa," Tate said, with a smile.

He'd shot both of those deer too low. They were close, so why didn't he make a killing shot? I was concerned about his gun being off, so I took it out and tried a few shots. The gun was right on target, not even a half inch off the bull's-eye. If anything, it might have been just a little high in close.

I recalled my first hunts with that .30-.30 lever action with the buckhorns sites. I got buck fever and wouldn't get to the bottom of the rear sites. I'd shoot high on the bucks every time. Tate was not taking enough of the front bead, causing him to shoot under them. Maybe it was a genetic thing like big noses run in some families. I'd have to work on him for next year.

10

TATE BAGS ANOTHER ONE

The following year rolled around, and Tate was busy with school plays, so we didn't go out bow hunting. Instead, Floyd and I hunted McCoy in the early fall with our crossbows. If my memory serves me right, we shot a small buck and a doe.

Tate missed the opening weekend of the gun hunt. He had another commitment for school. Finally, on Thanksgiving, he came along with us. We hunted in the middle of the north post. Fresh snow was falling, and you could walk without making a sound.

I knew a spot where deer holed up in heavy weather. It was just over a small hill out of sight from the roadway. I told Tate to take the lead; I used my walking sticks and followed him. We were just about to the top of an oak ridge.

"Tate, hold up." I put my finger to my mouth, motioning for him to come to me.

He came over, whispering to me, "What's up, Grandpa?"

"I'm going to wait here. You go very, very slowly to

the top of the hill. You're just going to peek over the ridge. If deer are there, they'll be laying in the thick bush about halfway down the hill."

"OK, Grandpa, I've got it."

He stalked up the hill like a pro. It was so good to see him learning the sport. When he got to the top of the hill, he stopped and motioned to me that there was a deer. I nodded my head for him to take his shot. He carefully aimed, taking a shot.

For a few minutes, he just stood there looking into the valley below. I tried to get up the slippery hill behind him, with little success. Finally, he came back to help me with the steep grade. "Did you get one?"

"Grandpa, I think I hit one, there were two of them, but the deer seemed to disappear.

"OK, we'll take a look. Where did you shoot it? Remember, I taught you to pick out a tree or something to mark the deer position."

"Well, the deer was just below that pine tree when I shot. Both deer were lying down."

I carefully went down the grade, with Tate in the lead. I cautioned him to keep his gun ready. When we got to the area, there was no sign of blood. The brush was heavy. Just a short distance down the hill, I thought I spotted blood.

When I walked in that direction, I saw no deer. For some reason, the military at Fort McCoy had dug holes in the ground behind this hill. It might have been soldiers digging a place to hide their beer cans. Who knows? Was that doe down in one of those holes? As I approached the area, a deer head popped out of one of the depressions.

I shot the deer to end its life. I saw that both front legs were broken when we pulled the doe out of the hole. He'd hit the deer too low. It was right on target but two inches too low. I congratulated him. "Great hunt there, young fellow. You stalked those deer like a Native American Indian."

He was rightfully proud of himself. We took a photo on his cell phone and sent it home to Mom. Things were getting very wet in the woods. Grandpa was ready for a warm fire. We gutted the doe while screaming for Floyd to come. He had already gone to the truck and must have heard the shot. In a few minutes, he showed up.

"Who shot that nice doe?"

I saw Tate smile from the corner of my eye. "I did, Uncle Floyd, but she doesn't have any nuts to eat."

"Well, would a couple of tits be all right?

"No, it has to be nuts."

"OK, it has to be nuts."

As we pulled the doe back to the truck, the woods got prettier by the minute. The wet snow hung on the trees like Christmas garland. As you looked west, the flakes flowed over the trees like a waterfall. What a beautiful day to remember. But of course, the day belonged to Tate. I was just there to build up my storage of memories.

The very last hunt I took with Tate was the following year. We were hunting along the west side of

Fort McCoy. We were right across the road from Dick Smith's cabin. Dick was a rebellious guy, giving Fort McCoy the finger whenever he could find something to bitch about. Of course, they sometimes deserved it, but he took it to the extreme.

The fort did their best to be good neighbors to the community. But of course we were talking about the army here. If you ever worked for them, you know many small thinkers have eaten their way to the top of the shit pile. I believe Dick was smart enough to feed off that climate.

This morning was a little snappy out; the hair in your nose froze. I sat Tate on a hill looking to the south. He would be above the deer trail that came from the road. So I just walked over the rise to watch to the north.

I sat there for maybe forty-five minutes when a boom came from Tate's stand. Then another shot went off. I got my rifle ready, but nothing came. So I sat there for a couple of minutes. Then, finally, I decided to look at what the boy had.

When I got there, Tate was down below in the valley, searching for blood in the snow. I went to help him look. After a few minutes, we found blood. Not a lot of blood for the caliber of the gun.

"Tate, what was it?"

"Grandpa, it was a nice eight-point buck with two doe."

I could tell he was sick about not dropping him in place. "Well, let's see what we can find," I said.

We tracked him to the road. I found part of his nut sack about fifty feet across the road. Once again, he'd shot too low. "Tate, at least you have the nut sack. You can get a coin purse made out of it."

We tracked the buck up a hill behind Dick Smith's cabin. The blood was starting to stop. At the top of the hill, I decided we'd better go back. I didn't want to get in trouble with the pseudobiologist from Cataract.

Those boys are related to the PBS from Wilton. Never know what they might do to a couple of pretty boys from the big city of Tomah. Floyd came along and took the hill down away with no success in finding the buck. Tate hunted with me for three years and shot a deer every year. He damn near took an excellent buck on this hunt.

I will never forget those hunts with him. I'm sure he will also remember hunting deer with Grandpa. But unfortunately, I fear that younger men will never get the opportunity to hunt with their grandchildren.

Then the fact that only land barons' children can hunt further complicates the process. Hunting used to be a poor man's sport. It's now only for the rich.

Moreover, land has inflated, so even the present owner will be forced out by big money from the outside.

The rich folks from affluent communities in our nation have already brought up many farms. They control access to the once locally owned family farms.

The only way to save hunting for the poor would be to make all wildlands public owned. Do the deer belong to the people, or do they belong to just the landowners?

The answer is that deer belong to the people. That question leads to another observation about land. Land usage requires careful planning. Farms can be planted or pastured.

In contrast, more land should be set aside as natural areas. What if the public owned all the natural areas on farms?

Grandfathers could take a walkabout with their grandchildren to enjoy the wild. Every man would have a claim on the rough country—what a wonderful place Wisconsin would be for our grandchildren to grow up in.

One of the reasons I stopped hunting on Fort McCoy was that a PB squad had formed. I believe they were related to the PB from Wilton, Cataract, and Warrens. The fort had a small thinker for a commander, who liked to hunt deer.

Range control goons hatched a plan to keep hunters out of the land adjacent to a firing range. Then the commander's family and the goons would hunt that area.

He thought he had the right to set aside a hunting reserve for himself. After all, who is going to challenge the king of the goons? I wanted to give him an award for being the most significant prick ever to take command of Fort McCoy.

I wished I'd exposed the cockroach to the press or written a letter to higher headquarters questioning the boy's authority. How would that letter have looked in his promotion packet?

It might have been the next commander who

decided to register hunter's rifles. But of course, these boys couldn't help themselves from meddling with the deer hunts.

But what in the hell was he thinking? There never was a threat from deer hunters at the fort.

The two killings I can remember were committed by soldiers. One active-duty soldier killed one of my neighbors for running around with his wife.

It was one of those Hiawatha Golf Club romances. My neighbor was finding a hole in one of the army wives. Her husband went off the deep end and put a hole in him. It happens. Sad, but shit happens!

The other was a veteran just out of the military who accidentally killed a guy. I believe some guys were either drunk or high and screwing around with guns. One guy pointed a loaded gun at the other and pulled the trigger.

Ouch, that hurt. Private citizens have much more to fear from soldiers than hunters. Another pain in the ass was the police department at Fort McCoy. They had nothing to do and were looking to gain power over someone.

For many years they had a respected game warden. The fort decided to let the regular police force enforce hunting rules. They didn't know the laws. They didn't even know what areas were open or closed. If you asked them a question, they would be right about 50 percent of the time. They were too lazy or incompetent to do the job.

They added new rules every year that made no sense. My take on it is that they needed better officers.

I'd also pick my commanding officer from the top of the apple tree. For Christ's sake, most police officers and goons pissed their pants until they were twelve years old.

Colonel Moran was the best commander I ever served under. He knew to put the ass kissers in their place. But unfortunately, when they went over to the reserve command structure, things went south.

A good commander surrounds himself with qualified people. He set goals for the base, then allows skilled managers to run the place right.

My commander in Vietnam would have taken a bullet for any of his men. He was respected by the men that served under him. He began to tear up when he pinned the Bronze Star and Purple Heart on me in the field hospital.

Real leaders do not bend the rules to massage their overblown egos. They wouldn't think of association with assholes with weak bladders. They don't need goons telling them they have the most extended Jonnie in the crowd. It's a privilege to lead men, earned, not awarded. Enough about Fort McCoy, Kim. You'll get this, FTA.

My wife, Shi, and I decided to build our dream house on the western side of the Hiawatha Golf Course. We'd worked hard for years and finally saved enough money to build our dream.

It was next to Laura and Brendan Smith's home. I got to know Brendan pretty well, and we became friends. He also was a combat veteran, serving in the sand wars. He had some land in the Warrens area and invited me to hunt his property.

He even built a lovely tree stand for me to sit in. He is a good, respectful man with the right attitude toward leadership. Being a veteran himself, he understands what I had to go through.

I've poked a couple of deer on his property. He helped me more than once with the rascals. He has taken a few bucks himself. He shot one with a bow and the other with a gun. I'm sure he'll score a good buck sooner or later.

On one of our gun hunts, a once-in-a-lifetime buck came close to getting shot. The buck came into the woods with three does and a six-point buck from the west.

My brother Floyd shot at the six-point buck before the big buck arrived. But, unfortunately, that made the big buck circle wide of him.

He came down through a thick pine plantation. I never saw him until he cleared the end of it. I was too far away and didn't have time to scope him. He ran across the road up a driveway, disappearing in the thick cover. I didn't know how big he was, but I knew he was big.

About a half hour later, a truck pulled into Brendan's place. The guy that owned the cranberry marsh got out and came over. He asked, "Did you get that big boy? I want to take a look at him if you did."

I replied, "No, I saw him but never got a shot. It was my brother that shot at a six-point buck. He missed him and screwed up his chance at the big buck. How big was he?"

The guy was just sick over it. He began, "I was sitting in my stand when the herd came through. When I turned to get a shot, the seat on the stand squeaked. That is all it took. They picked me up, and I never got a shot. He was the biggest buck I've ever seen in my life. Had dropped tines, a huge rack, I'm talking huge."

"That's a shame." I told him the story of the buck I missed as a young hunter. "That's hunting. What can go wrong more than likely will. At least you have the memories to comfort you. He's still running. You might get another chance at him."

Floyd is eighty years old, and we hunted Brendan's place last year on an opening day. We had an excellent breakfast sitting around his wood stove. It was just about light, so Floyd went around to his stand. I had to wait a few minutes before going to my stand. We did this in case I kicked something out to him.

Brendan and I waited for a while before going to our stands. I thought I saw a buck cross the fire lane as I walked to my stand. I guess the buck just went into the pines and stopped. In about a half hour, I heard Floyd shoot. *Interesting,* I thought.

Around eight, a doe herd came right under my stand with their fawns. I could have shot, but I let the deer pass by. I was satisfied to watch them. It was less than an hour before a good-size deer came through.

He ran at a pretty good clip, moving away from me all the while. When he cleared the brush line, I saw he had one horn. I was ready, but I couldn't get him in the scope. I thought he might go right to Floyd, but he went across the fence line to another farm.

Floyd came around the pine trees smiling, and I knew he'd got one. I climbed down and went to see what he had. Floyd had shot a nice eight-point buck right between the eyes at one hundred yards. I knew where he was sitting; boys, it was a hundred-yard shot.

The buck was the one I saw early in the day crossing into the pines. He was just walking down the fire lane right to Floyd's stand. The buck picked up Floyd's scent or image at one hundred yards. He was ready to bolt, so Floyd took good aim and shot. What a wonderful memory for a man that age to take to heaven with him.

Neither Brendan nor I took a buck that day. Brendan didn't see anything, and I let one get away. The deer have been smartening up in that area. They make few mistakes and know the location of every deer stand in the woods. They even know when someone is sitting in them.

I would have stopped hunting years ago if it weren't for a few friends and my brother Floyd. Thanks to Brendan and Laura Smith for the many evenings I watched the sundown on your beautiful farm, and thanks to Kim Mello for developing a handicapped hunt at Fort McCoy.

11

MY LAST HUNT

The western skyline had just swallowed the ghost moon on this cool October morning. Looking to the east, I could see the sun hiding just below the earth's curvature. Brilliant red and orange lights announced the coming of a new day. In less than a minute, the sun peeked over the horizon. Narrow shafts of light bore their way through the stands of hardwood trees. Morning had broken on the Tar Valley Wilderness Road.

The air was still, with low clouds of ground fog hugging the valleys bordering the Wilderness Road. The road carefully straddled the valleys, keeping its feet dry on the crest of the hill. It was mid-October, and the raw beauty of the hardwood forest teased for my attention.

Quietly, I navigated the washboard ruts in the old road. Passing a spring pond, I noticed ice crystals resembling pearl earrings hanging from ferns. Unfortunately, the ferns had carelessly tempted jack frost one too many times.

The sound of water chirping as it erupted from a spring told me I had arrived at my hunt. I slowed my pace, knowing my approach to the deer stand must be without sound. A ruffed grouse flushed from a sumac thicket as I took my first few steps off the road.

The tip of the grouse wing struck a milkweed pod. Blooms of white cotton exploded into the air. I watched as the cotton disappeared into the cover. I wondered, *Will this be my last hunt?*

As I prepared to set up my watch, I see a lone drake wood duck sitting on the pond. The early morning light had given the pond a mirror-like appearance. But, hm, is the reflection the duck or the duck the reflection?

The forest was quiet. Many of the songbirds had left for the season. My mind was flooded with memories of picking raspberries along this road as a child. My older brother, Jim, and I would gather enough berries for a pie. Usually, we weren't successful. One look at our purple-stained tongues gave the reason for our failure.

We had found crude Indian arrowheads not too far from this road. We wondered what this land looked like when the Ho-Chunk braves hunted here. We'd imagined ourselves as Ho-Chunk braves riding our spotted ponies with a whitetail buck slung over a pack pony.

A flash of movement on the adjacent hillside brought me back to this day. With no sudden movement, I prepared my bow for firing. The huge fourteen-point buck came within range. The arrow was ready for a killing shot. A voice that seemed to come from the buck spoke.

"Do you remember my grandfather?"

Slowly, I brought the bow back to rest. The buck turned, making eye contact with me.

"Remember the white grass field you and your uncle Hipe watched a beautiful buck run across?"

"Yes, are you that buck I saw over fifty years ago?"

The buck answered, "He was one of my great-grandfathers."

I said, "That was a lifetime ago. Why have you come to me now?"

"I'm here to pass along the knowledge of our ancestors to you. Man must understand that our mother is the creator of all things. You are the one to carry the message. Are you ready to receive the blessing?"

"I'm seventy-four years old. Wouldn't a younger man be a better choice?"

"No, they aren't ready to watch, listen, and learn the teachings of the wild."

"I'll do my best to remember what you teach me."

"Better yet, write it down in a book," the buck said.

I dug a pencil and paper out of my pack bag. I leaned against an oak tree. "OK, I'm ready."

The wind began to blow, forming small wind tunnels of leaves, sticks, and dirt. Then holograms of wolves appeared in the tunnels. Sounds of whimpers from wolf pups filled the air. As the volume increased, it sounded more like they were crying.

"Why are the pups crying?" I asked.

"Reach out and touch one of them," the buck replied.

I touched one of the pups, which stopped spinning and morphed into a bald eagle. It had a crushed eggshell in its talons. "I do not understand what you are showing me."

"That's fine; it will become clear to you. Touch a few more of the pups."

I raised my hand and touched two more spinning pups. One morphed into a Karner blue butterfly sitting on a stalk of a wild lupine plant. The other morphed into a black-footed ferret head with the body of a prairie dog.

I asked, "Aren't these animals on the endangered list?"

"Yes, they were."

"OK, why does the prairie dog have the head of a ferret?"

"Look closely. Do you see what the eagle is carrying and what the Karner blue butterfly is sitting on?"

I answer, "Yes, an eggshell and a wild lupine plant."

The buck said, "The eagles were almost extinct in Monroe County because humankind had poisoned their food source with DDT. This poisoning caused the eggshells to be too thin to support the embryo's development. Do you know what plant Karner blue butterflies feed on?"

"No, I don't."

"Well, Karner blue butterflies feed on wild lupine plants. The black-footed ferret feeds on prairie dogs. Prairie dogs are visited by the plague, which ferrets can also get. Is that connection clear for you?"

"Yes, it is."

I looked up to see hundreds of wolf pups spinning in circles around me. "Does each one of these pups represent an endangered animal?"

"Some represent animals, others plants. In nature, both are of equal importance. One cannot be kept in balance without the other." Sitting back against an old oak tree, I pondered what this buck had shown me. I asked, "How can an old man like me help to keep nature in balance?"

"You have to think about land differently. Man has incorrectly divided Monroe County into towns, roads, and farms owned by different people. Ask yourself, how did our mother divide the county? She divided it into small ecosystems called watersheds.

"Animals rely on their watershed or neighboring watersheds for food and shelter. Therefore, you must concentrate on the watershed's health to keep plants and creatures healthy."

"I believe I understand what I need to do to save these animals and plants from extinction."

"Hold on. There is more I haven't taught you."

"What's that?" I asked.

"The Monroe County pseudobiologist will visit you. They'll come in anger and shoot from their lips, but their minds are capable of understanding. So, you have to teach them."

"I will do my best to convey our mother's needs. I honor you. Thank you for bringing that message to me."

"You cannot do your work alone, so please listen to their concerns. The only answer is to teach all humankind to care for our mother. The animals and plants depend on you to take care of them. The most important question is, who does the land belong to?"

"Is the answer our mother?" I questioned.

"Yes, nature is not one man's possession. A man's role is caretaker, not the owner of the land. Conversation requires support from insightful caretakers able to think beyond their greed and lives. Teach them to wear their velvet moccasins when treading in our wilderness. If they stare into the forests they've just walked in, they should see no evidence of intrusion."

A bald eagle exploded into flight over the buck's head. The buck disappeared into the clouds. The wind started to blow harder; it kept getting stronger.

I said, "I will do my best, but I'm still not sure it will be enough."

Grandfather replied, "Don't worry, Grandmother and I will help you."

12

THE WATERSHED

I turn to see several all-terrain vehicles boring down on me. The vehicles were ridden by skeletons wearing baseball caps on backward. They have Sorel hunting boots on, with diapers covering their privates. On the side of one of the ATVs, I read Monroe County Pseudo-biologist. They circled me, constantly glaring and giving me the finger.

They have tattoos on their bones. One guy's tattoo on his skull reads, COVID-19 is a lie. Another one has a tattoo on the ribcage that reads, Smoking is good for you. Probably they died from those diseases. One has a pink camouflage diaper; she must have been a woman who died of cancer.

This gang must be the bunch the buck told me to expect. The gang kept getting closer with each circle the ATVs made. Finally, they stopped, and the gang's king got off his machine. He walked around to the back of his ATV and pulled a knife from his back pocket.

Teachings from the Buddha came to me. I said,

"Hear these words from Buddha: You will not be punished for your anger. Your anger will punish you."

The king scratched his pubic bone and stared at me, saying, "I knew Bubba all my life, and he never said that. I'm not impressed. If you have something to say, just come out with it."

I remembered a teaching from a bible class I took many years ago. I told them the bible tells us about conservation, from Job 12:7–10:

But ask the animals, and they will teach you, or the birds of the air, and they will tell you; or speak to the earth, and it will teach you, or let the fish of the sea inform you. Which of all these does not know that the hand of the LORD has done this? In His hand is the life of every creature and the breath of all mankind.

They still didn't understand what I was trying to convey. So I took a few minutes to allow the great spirit of my grandfather to fill my mind with the right thoughts. Then, a quote from John Madison came to me.

"Through almost all human existence, hunt-able land and hunt-able wildlife have preceded the hunter. They caused the hunter. But in the future, this must be reversed. It is the hunter who must cause hunt-able land and wildlife. And a world worth bringing young into."

Finally, I could see I'd piqued their interest. The quote might help me with my opportunity to tell my story, so I began. "In the years I've hunted in Monroe County, there has been the destruction of the sport as I knew it. Certainly, the attitudes about the ownership of deer will have to change. The next generation of Americans will have to come to the wild places to give, not to take."

The king interrupted me. "I can't believe all that. I'm a republican and don't believe in global warming."

The pack of gray wolves howled. Looking around, the gang noticed hundreds of wolves surrounding them. Like a herd of muskoxen with horns pointing out, the members pulled out their long rifles.

I raised my hand to settle them. Once again, the wolves howled. This time it sounded more like a cry.

The king asked, "Why are the wolves crying?"

I said, "They are crying about their losses."

The king shouted back, "Those damn wolves are the reason the deer numbers are down. We need to kill all of them."

I replied, "Wolves preyed on buffalo for thousands of years. When your great-grandfather settled in this country, there were thirty to sixty million buffalo. After we settled the country, there were twenty-three buffalo left in Pelican Valley of central Yellowstone."

"So what's that got to do with anything?" the king said.

I said, "Buffalo were a keystone species, which control the environment they live in. Wolves didn't overpopulate and kill all the buffalo. They kept the herd in check. If the wolves hadn't been in the system, buffalo would have eaten their way out of a home."

The king said, "So, buffalo are keystone species?"

I replied, "Yes, a keystone species is a species that has a disproportionately large impact on its environment. They hold ecosystems together and support biodiversity."

"That makes no sense to me. Why aren't the wolves the keystone species?" the king said.

"I'll give you a present-day example of what I'm trying to convey. In Africa, wildebeest numbers declined because of disease. With the reduction in the wildebeest population, the grass flourished, creating more fuel for fires. These fires prevent young trees from growing.

"Then, predators declined, along with many other animals. In a few years, the wildebeest herd recovered. They ate the grasses, which prevented fires. With less fuel for the fires, trees started to grow again.

"What happened next is truly amazing. Biologists are starting to see elephants and giraffes on the landscape. They witnessed an improvement in the numbers of all grassland grazers, which triggered a return of lions and hyenas, natural predators."

The king said, "So, the wildebeest was the keystone species in that case?"

"Yes, the wildebeest was the glue that held the whole system together."

Some wolves were growling, showing their teeth, while others were wagging their tails, appearing content. "Why is that?" the king asked.

I answered, "These wolves represent a plant or animal native to Monroe County. See those two playing with each other? One represents wild turkeys and the other bald eagles. Both species have been brought back from extinction in the county."

"I understand animal extinction is a problem, but what do plants have to do with anything?"

"Plants are the foundation for the health of all animals. If we don't take care of the plants, animals will not exist. It all starts with the watersheds."

"Watersheds? I'm not following your thinking."

"Yes, the land in a healthy watershed converts energy from the sunlight into plants that support animals, a process called photosynthesis. The watershed acts like a nursery for plants, which feeds insects, right?"

"OK, I know that."

"Say a monarch butterfly lays an egg on a milkweed plant, which develops into a caterpillar, then a butterfly. Now, some intelligent old birds know this and feed on the caterpillars.

"Finally, a bobcat sees a lazy bird sitting too low in a tree. The bobcat springs into action. Guess what's for lunch today? This chain of consumption is necessary to balance our ecosystem."

I noticed that one of the skeletons was wearing a traditional Native American wampum belt. I might make more progress with him, so I asked, "Are you from the Cherokee tribe?"

"Yes, how did you know?"

"From the wampum belt you're wearing. Are you a shaman?"

"No, but my grandfather was."

"What's your name?"

"Stanley."

"Stanley, I'll bet you know why the wolf still cries, don't you?"

"I have a pretty good idea. Is it because man has not taken care of the land? Which caused global warming that ended up threatening all life on earth with extinction?"

"Exactly. Ask yourself, would your people support the extinction of any animal or plant? Wouldn't they want you to help restore air, water, and land? Then all of the creatures, including man, would be in the correct orbit in the watershed. Do you imagine that controlling the whitetail deer will solve the destruction of the wild?"

"No, it won't, and I'm ashamed of my behavior. You have my apology. How can I help set the table for every creature on this planet to have a meal with me? I'm not sure where to start."

"Start by supporting organizations like the Mississippi Valley Conservancy. Their organization works with landowners to set aside land for the ones that will inherit our planet."

Stanley asked, "Did you study how nature works in school?"

"No, I learned much of it from sitting in the forest with To ya and Wi ya ha."

"Your parents," the king interjected.

"Well, they are all of our grandparents," I said.

"I know I'm not related to you," the king said.

"Please let me finish. The Cherokee Indian spiritual

legend has it that the moon is Grandfather (To ya) and the sun is Grandmother (Wi ya ha). She sees everything that happens on earth. She controls the four spirit messenger winds. The winds are messengers, spiritual beings, which mind the movement of the sun, earth, and stars."

Stanley said, "Lately, I've felt something was wrong with the messenger winds; they've been restless."

"That's a warning sign, Stanley. If man continues to abuse the earth, they will destroy all humankind. Do you remember the story of the three sisters?"

"Yes, it was told to me by my grandfather."

"Would you please share it with the rest of the gang?"

Stanley sat on an oak stump and began. "The story of the three sisters came down from my elders. My grandparents would plant beans, corn, and squash on one hill. The three plants all did well growing together.

"The cornstalk serves as a trellis for the beans to climb. Next, the beans fix nitrogen in the soil, and their twining vines stabilize the maize in high winds. Then broad leaves of the squash plant shade the ground. Finally, they kept the earth moist and helped prevent the establishment of weeds."

"Stanley, our mother should never be left naked. She must be covered with a blanket knitted together from native plants. What if Native Americans and modern-day scientists taught landowners in Monroe County how to dress our mother? I'm sure the watersheds would start to heal themselves."

Stanley said, "Many people live in town and only have small lots. How can they help?"

"Those lots are still in a watershed. What if they planted their lots with the plants to support the watershed? They would be assisting the Mississippi Valley Conservancy without ever leaving the backyard."

"What if the large landowners refuse to listen?"

"I'm sure they won't listen. My thoughts are that large landowners of Monroe County should be regulated by the people. Those resources belong to all the citizens."

Stanley said, "Large landowners would never agree to that."

"It takes one hundred to two hundred years to build one inch of topsoil. That is longer than any of them will live. No one even knows how long it will take to restore groundwater aquifers to a pristine state."

"What is the answer?" Stanley asked.

"Many farmers in this country choose to practice sustainable farming methods. Sustainable farming needs to be mandatory, not a choice. Take out a dollar bill and hold it close to your eyes."

Stanley did.

"Can you see anything other than the money?"

"No, I can't."

"Stanley, now move the money away from your eyes a little."

Stanley did.

"Now, what do you see?"

"Well, I see the animals, a stream, the sky, the entire watershed."

"Stanley, your ancestors knew what I'm telling you to be true. Did any Native Americans have a deed to their land? So, yes, it's possible. When I listen to a Native American play a flute, I can hear the messenger winds crying for help."

"Thanks, you've touched my heart," Stanley said.

I've done my best to spread the message to the County of Monroe. I wondered if it would be enough to change the residents' minds. I said silently, "Grandfather, how did I do?"

13

MY GRANDPARENTS VISIT

Grandfather's voice came from me, but my lips did not move. The voice spooked the group, and they pulled back. To ya spoke softly to calm their fears.

Speaking to no one person, he began. "Humans have carelessly altered their environment at the expense of the planet. As a result, natural systems were destroyed in the name of progress. This unbalancing of systems caused many creatures to disappear. In some areas, even the tiny ribbons of the wild country were destroyed.

"Stanley shares with you the story of the three sisters. I will now try to connect the three sisters' story to the watersheds. Watersheds are our grandmother's children. Millions of years ago, she gave birth to them. They store the secrets needed for life to flourish. The DNA of the plants and animals living in the watersheds constantly evolves.

"Each of her children has instructions on how to succeed. All plants of the watershed compete with one another for the right to live. The most successful plants in adapting to the environment of the watershed dominate, while less adaptive plants die out. That's why invasive plants are so harmful to a pristine watershed.

"All plants pump energy from the sun to the roots. As they do, carbon is absorbed into the earth. This action purifies the air. Mother has given them large root systems to stabilize the soil and absorb the rainwater. Scientists have developed plants for high yields with small root systems. Those plants mostly take from the watershed.

"Mother knew that keeping as much water as possible where it fell to earth was very important. Some storms deliver more water than the plants can absorb. After a rain the forest holds the water then slowly uses it. Mother created depressions in the earth to hold the excess water. Wetlands absorb the excessive flow, then slowly disperse water to the ground table.

"The growth of plant life summons the pollinator, such as bees and butterflies, to join the dance. Plants emit chemicals to protect themselves from destruction. Insects adapt their digestive system to digest these chemicals. Forever plants on earth, Mother has created a predator.

"Animals also are predators of plants and each other. This is the way Mother balances nature. Native Americans learned to interact with plants and animals. This gave them the insight necessary to take care of the earth.

"Unlike the kings that rule the watershed nowadays, they coexisted with the watershed—honoring and protecting the watershed for the generations that would follow."

The king said, "This sounds like liberal democratic crap to me. I'm a republican and don't believe in global warming, COVID shots, or indigenous people's rights."

Grandfather replied, "I don't care what tribe you're from. Why do you feel the need to label yourself and me? I'm not a democratic or a republican. I'm your grandfather."

The king shouted, "You're not my Grandfather. You're a stinking Indian."

Grandfather realized he could not reach the king. I could feel his disappointment. Yet, he did not step into the trap of anger the king had set. "Your ignorance does not serve you well. Hear these words from Chief Seattle."

The king asked, "Who's ignorant?"

Grandfather said, "The earth does not belong to man. Man belongs to the earth. All things are connected like the blood that unites us all. Man did not weave the web of life, and he is merely a strand in it. Whatever he does to the web, he does to himself."

As Grandfather finished that quote, I felt him leave my body. It was quiet for a few minutes. Then, a flute started playing gently in the background. I knew Wi ya ha, my grandmother's voice, would come soon. She thought surely they would listen to the looming threat to the planet.

Wi ya ha began. "You need to know that the warning signs are all around you. I've sent the messenger winds to alert you. Didn't you notice the winds pushing against their brothers when the season changed? This is an explosive dance, creating thunder, lighting, and rain.

Usually, they push each other back and forward, but occasionally they will begin to spin. This is when they can destroy everything in their path.

Unfortunately, global warming has strengthened its grip, and it's much harder for me to control them—resulting in much more flooding and damage to our planet.

"Then, there are the times when their hot breath burns the land to a cinder, setting the stage for fires that are so powerful they create weather systems."

Wi ya ha stopped for a few minutes, and the wind picked up. "I ask you, Can you not hear the truth that I speak?" There was silence for a few minutes.

Then, the king spoke. "All I can hear is the wind blowing. You're another tree-hugging democrat like your husband."

Wi ya ha replied, "I'm yours, and Grandmother to all of the planet's people."

The king shouted back in a raised voice, "I'm not your grandson."

The flute stopped playing, and Grandmother addressed his refusal to listen. "You could not hear the truth from the Great Spirit, your grandfather. So now, you reject the truth from your grandmother."

"You're not my grandmother."

"Hear this warning, and if you destroy the watershed, you destroy yourself. I've woven the forest, rocks, plants, streams, and animals together for a reason. Native Americans were one with the planet. You are a stranger to your own body and the watershed."

"So, you say," the king replied.

"Whites like you walk in the shadows of ignorance. The heat from my fires does not burn them. They cannot feel the winds I've sent to warn them. Their ears do not understand the language of the Native American elders. They stumble along the path of darkness without recognizing the environmental damage. Man's window of opportunity will soon disappear into the night. I shed my tears for America, for it is the twilight time of our nation."

The king replied, "Whites rule this nation."

I could see this was not going anywhere. The king could not understand that we all are part of the watershed family. I said, "Grandmother, maybe if I change the conversation to concentrate on deer hunting, he'll understand."

"Well, try if you may," she replied, with this poem, as I felt her slip away from me:

Born in Monroe County.
Shown Grandmother's beauty your entire life.
Still, ignorance was the path you stumbled along.
Grandmother sent messenger winds to warn;
they didn't ruffle you.

Grandmother sent fires to warn; they didn't burn you.
Grandmother sent Native American elders to warn;
they didn't convince you.

Grandmother came herself, "and still, you refuse to listen?"

My body and my voice returned to normal. However, I could see the king was upset and needed me to put it in terms he could understand.

I said, "I picked up some information about deer management reading the bottom of beer cans from the Budweiser beer company. So someday, when you have a flashlight handy, shine it down an empty beer can. The secrets of deer management are on the bottom inside the can."

"I have looked down beer cans all my life and never seen any messages. I have a flashlight in my saddlebags. Just wait a minute." The king screamed at Angel, one of the gang members, "You lazy Mexican, get me a Budweiser beer." So Angel went to retrieve a Budweiser for the king.

I said, "Now that I think about it, I believe it was the Corona beer company with the messages."

"That's not a problem. We are out of Budweiser," Angel said as he pulled a cold Corona from the ice cooler. "We have plenty of Corona."

Thinking quickly, I said, "Well, that won't work. You can only see the message while also smoking Mexican weed."

Pulling an assault rifle from his ATV, the king said, "We have plenty of Mexican weed, and I'm a Republican."

I stop him at *Republican.* "And nothing anyone says will convince you that your jerkwater, closed-minded attitude prevents you from seeing the truth. In truth, you're a RINO. Real Republicans drink Scottish whisky and are smart enough to trick Budweiser-drinking RINOs into voting for them."

"What did you call me?" the king said as he raised his assault rifle and aimed at me.

"I called you a RINO: Republican In Name Only. Don't shoot. Would the term *Truth Denier* be better? Allow me to recite this quote from former vice president Al Gore." Those were my last words. The king fired his assault rifle.

I would tell him, "This is not a political issue. This is a moral issue. It affects the survival of human civilization. It is not a question of left vs. right; it is a question of right vs. wrong. But, it is wrong to destroy the habitability of our planet and ruin the prospects of every generation that follows ours."

When I awoke, I was above the tree line. I could see the entire county of Monroe. There were no towns, farms, or even a road. The land was pristine, and the woods were filled with wild game. My amputated leg had grown back, and I felt like a young man again. A circle of men surrounded me—my grandfather, Dad, Uncle Hipe, best friend Bill, and all my brothers were in the ring.

Grandfather said, "The king believes the *Republican* tribe members are somehow different from the *Democratic* tribe members. Using political ideology, he has become a *Truth Denier.* He has built a society so removed from his grandparents he no longer recognizes them. If any man does not recognize his grandparents, he is truly lost."

Dad spoke up, "Stop dillydallying around and get your gun. We're going to make a drive."

"Dad, I'd like to take a walkabout today. How would it be if Grandfather and I just hunted together today?" May these words by Aldo Leopold about killing a wolf in his early years touch your heart?

We reached the old wolf in time to watch a fierce green fire dying in her eyes. I realized then, and have known ever since, that there was something new to me in those eyes — something known only to her and the mountain. I was young then and full of trigger itch; I thought that because fewer wolves meant more deer, no wolves would mean hunters' paradise. But after seeing the green fire die, I sensed that neither the wolf nor the mountain agreed with such a view.

A couple of beautiful biologists I've had the privilege of calling friends spend their entire lives drying Mother's tears. Their names are Kim Mello and Kurt Brownell. In recognition of their commitment to Monroe County, I reserve my autograph of this book to organizations raising funds to reclaim the wild places in Wisconsin.

May God bless my wife, Shi, sons Shawn and Steve, daughters Jennifer and Emily, and grandson Tate. Love you all.

EPILOGUE

In my lifetime, deer hunting has become a sport controlled by landowners who worship the concept of
managing deer for the size of their horns. If they would
look to Native American elders for guidance, they
would undoubtedly consider a strategy similar to Wa
ya ha and To ya's plan.

One questions the landowner's expertise in deer
management. Mother Nature manages prey animals
with predators. Would we be wise to mimic Mother
Nature? In the past, deer numbers were kept in balance
by increased predators or vice versa.

Predators took weak deer first, leaving a healthy deer
herd behind. In some counties in our state, 40 percent
of the deer harvested have the chronic wasting disease.
Have landowner's attempts to manage deer fostered an
out-of-control unhealthy deer herd?

A deer's gut has microbes, bacteria, fungi, viruses,
and their genes. These bacteria in the microbiome help
digest their food, regulate their immune system, and
protect against other bacteria that cause disease.

Deer evolved to eat natural plants from healthy watersheds. Healthy plants grow from the soil with a balanced microbiome. A balanced microbiome in soil comes from good management of sustainable watersheds.

What happens when contaminated feed is fed to cows? They get mad cow disease. Is it too much of a leap to believe deer could get sick similarly? Does feeding deer unnaturally change the microbiome in their gut, making them susceptible to disease?

It can be challenging to watch wolves take down a deer. Nature is seldom kind. Just remember they were the original managers of deer. Aldo Leopold put it best: "Only the mountain has lived long enough to listen objectively to the howls of the wolf."

Landowners must play the long game and manage the watershed, not the deer. Landowners are killing their mother for a set of large horns over the fireplace. Your goal should be to have a balanced ecosystem. Greed could be replaced with a connection to your grandparents.

Game farms are breeding grounds for disease if you're one to shoot an animal in a pen. Set a hunt up to shoot a beef cow in a barnyard. The Department of Natural Resources should close all game farms in Wisconsin and destroy all the animals inside. They go against all common sense.

How could change be accomplished with present-day politics? First, the Department of Natural

Resources needs to be removed from the control of the legislators in the state government. The legislators are influenced by greedy special interest groups, which leads to the mismanagement of our resources.

There has always been, and always will be, some particular interest group wanting to rape the resources for their gain. Their street name is shortstop. Managing our resources is a difficult job, best left to the people of science, not people playing the short game.

The solution to good deer management is not in a beer can's bottom. It is in the education of our land-owners; you need to understand the management of our watersheds. I will repeat this quote from Chief Seattle: "The earth does not belong to man, and man belongs to the earth. All things are connected like the blood that unites us all. Man did not weave the web of life. He is merely a strand in it. Whatever he does to the web, he does to himself."

For those who are blessed with artistic abilities—playwrights, authors, songwriters, painters, orators—please explore ways of raising awareness of the watersheds' problems. I encourage all caring people to let their voices be heard.

We've allowed greed and ignorance to ruin our watersheds. We have no time to waste; global warming is upon us. Leadership is needed to educate citizens about the looming disaster on our doorstep.

Except for the last few chapters, my stories are a historical record of hunting in Monroe County. I felt it best to write about real people that lived in Monroe County. Hopefully, my readers will be able to relate to the stories I share about local folks.

If you've hunted in this county for a long time, you know what I'm telling you is accurate. We must look to our Mother for truth and go to the wild places to give, not take. And don't ride that stupid ATV. Instead, please take it to the dump the next time you go, and leave it there.

On your walks in our beautiful forest, you'll hear the voices of nature singing in the wind and calling you by name, caressing you into submission. Listen carefully, and our Mother has a story to share with you. So walk softly, wearing your velvet moccasins.

Thank you kindly for allowing me to share my unconventional thoughts with you.

IN MEMORIAM

As I picked up my pen to write the last page of this book, I found out my niece, Linda Martin, had been diagnosed with brain cancer.

The family rallied around her, showing her our love. We prayed, hugged, kissed, and cried with her. But unfortunately, on December 19, 2022, we lost our precious Linda.

One asks themselves, in times like this, where is the

love of God? Why would our Holy Father allow this to happen?

My understanding of the teachings of the Bible is that God never said there wouldn't be suffering in our lives, but he said that if we believe in him, we will be with him in heaven forever. Linda, I know the Holy Father has you in his arms.

I know many families are suffering from the relentless killer cancer. Will it help to donate all the proceeds from this book to the cancer research in Linda's name? Yes. Then, maybe, in times to come, we can save all the ladies suffering with breast cancer.